DARLEYS IN THE DALE
ECHOES FROM THE VALLEY

LEWIS R JACKSON

COUNTRY BOOKS

Published by:
Country Books
Courtyard Cottage, Little Longstone, Bakewell, Derbyshire DE45 1NN

ISBN 1 898941 69 6

© 2002 Lewis R Jackson

Reprinted 2006

British Library in Cataloguing in Publication Data:
a catalogue record for this book is available from the British Library.

Printed and bound by Cromwell Press, Trowbridge, Wiltshire

CONTENTS

PREFACE   5

CHAPTER 1 THE VALLEY AND ITS SETTLEMENTS   9

CHAPTER 2 HISTORY   53

CHAPTER 3 COMMUNICATIONS, WATER AND POWER   92

CHAPTER 4 HEALTH AND HAPPINESS   121

CHAPTER 5 THE ECONOMY OF THE VALLEY   186

CHAPTER 6 LOCAL FIRMS   222

CHAPTER 7 MORE MEMORIES OF THE DALES   280

CHAPTER 8 WALKING TRAILS   298

ACKNOWLEDGEMENTS   319

BIBLIOGRAPHY   320

PREFACE

This book about Darley's past is not just a clinical reference gained through computer records. It includes knowledge acquired over the years I have lived in our valley.

Darley Dale is a most aptly named area. It is more than just a valley with a river flowing through it, it is a delight of Dales of all types. Dry limestone Dales sprinkled with thorn and ash, abundant with wild flowers growing on the sweet limestone soil, such as Northern Dale and Wensley Dale.

The Clough Brook Dale from Winster to Darley Bridge is an amazing area, with limestone on one side and gritstone on the other. It hosts a profusion of flora and fauna of all types. Two Dales' twin Dales of Ladygrove and Hall-Dale, with their cascading babbling brooks of crystal water set among gritstone rocks and an abundance of deciduous trees, are gems. Both these Dales have their beginnings on the wild moors on the east side of Darley, as does the Northwood Brook which is illuminated in the spring with drifts of bluebells glowing in the dappled sunshine filtering through the trees.

Little Rowsley's oddly named Smelting Wood brook is short and steep, leaping over a gritstone edge half as old as time. This majestic edge, which looms over the Derwent's eastern flanks on its journey from the Peak of Derbyshire, begins at Darley Dale

In my lifetime I have witnessed great change. From an age of innocence and contentment to an age of constant change and a 'must have' society. I mourn the loss of many things – social intimacy when one's neighbours were true neighbours; Darley Dale was just a scattered collection of rural hamlets; curlews' cries on the wild moors; a corncrake's rattling song; Stancliffe's sirens calling the quarry men to work, dressed in flat caps, big boots and corduroy trousers; railwaymen in leather caps and blue denim overalls and jackets; horse drivers and farmers in brown leather leggings; nursery men with spades and small hand tools; lead miners tramping over the fields and across the old Derwent footbridge to Millclose Mine; cows grazing the grass verges of country lanes, usually tended by the very young or the very old; Silver Service buses; timber drays and their magnificent shire horses; hay making with a horse-drawn waggon , tedders and rakes, pitch-forking sweet-smelling hay on to the dray and then the stack; gardens and allotments with an abundance of raspberries, strawberries and gooseberries, beans, peas and potatoes, and often a hen run; home-made jams, wines and nettle beer. The three farms which stretched from Northwood Lane to Two Dales along the east valley side now vanished, mostly replaced by tarmac and concrete dormitories or trees, where one's neighbours are unknown and often strangers to the valley. Celebrations at the Whitworth Institute and Park. Rail journeys and 'bus mystery trips. Sunday School outings and teas. Listening on a cold, still winter's night to the roaring, chuffing, clickety-click of the Manchester to London express, or the slow click, click, click of a goods train. Steam on misty nights reflecting the rosy glow from the open fire-box door. Steam engines, horses, fields, gardens and nurseries all had their own wonderful magical seasonal smells.

Wakes Week, Carnival Day, Christmas Day, seasonal games were full of expectation and excitement. Sitting in a neighbour's house listening to tales of yesterday, stories of families and the things they did. Long hot summer holidays spent picnicking, exploring and learning of things past and present in the valley. Watching out for rabbits, foxes, badgers, seeing occasional stoats and rats. A profusion of birds from pheasants to wrens. Nut trees, walnut, and chestnut trees and the beauty and mystery of the Ladygrove and Halldale brooks. Sledging in the winter nights by the light of ticking gas lamps. A horse-drawn triangular snow plough always kept at the top of Bent Lane near Burley Fields Farm. Following behind the huge shire horse and driver. Sometimes having the enormous thrill of a ride on the back of the snow-plough. It was to me a tranquil and safe valley, full of a myriad things to occupy every minute of every day. Long glorious days of contented bliss.

Over the years I have welcomed the coming of wireless, electricity, telephones, televisions and the ability to own a car or motor-cycle. An end to Monday washday drudgery, with dripping wet clothes hanging from the ceiling rack on wet winter days. No more very poor children going to school in the rain with a sack over their shoulders because they had no coats. The bliss of central heating and electric blankets. No more cold and wet dwellings. The chance to get to know the world through travel and television. Proper health care. No more infectious diseases – measles, scarlet fever and diptheria.

I dislike the "must have, should have" attitude of society today, the awareness of being unsafe, being too busy to spend time communing with nature and exploring our valley. Strange that in spite of all the material benefits that have come our way in the last century I believe that because our expectations are so much higher we have become more discontented, unsettled and isolated from our neighbours. When I was young time was there to be filled. Now we seem to have no time left to fill with the delights of our valley.

It is only approximately seventy-two generations ago since Roman soldiers stood on Oker Hill and gazed over the Darley valley. The last dozen generations of Darley people have seen more change than the sixty generations which preceded them could ever have imagined, especially the last two generations. The valley, its environment and the way of life of its dwellers has changed for ever. Its past is always present, its future is unknown. Our valley will endure for, and charm, many many more generations to come. I have been fortunate to have seen many valleys the world over but to me few could compare with our lovely Darley valley. Pendleton, in his book "A History of Derbyshire", sums up our valley perfectly.

"One of the fairest of Derbyshire haunts is Darley Dale. It stretches in peaceful, sylvan loveliness from Matlock up to Rowsley, where, dividing, the one arm, along which the Derwent flows, extends to and indeed beyond Chatsworth gates, and the other, through which the Wye winds, beyond Haddon Hall, up to Bakewell; and in whatever garb it appears, whether clothed in the bright freshness of spring, the rich glory of summer, the deep russet tints of autumn, or the hoar frost and feathery snow of winter, it is always beautiful. Like a pleasing tranquil face upon which ordinary troubles make no impress, it never loses its charm. But perhaps it is most inviting in the spring time, when the sunlight, coquetting with the Derwent, makes the river glisten like a streak of silver, when, the "gold of the buttercup and the green of the grass" mingle, in the fertile meadows, and the hedges are powdered with sweet-smelling hawthorne". The description is just as apt today as it was in 1886.

CHAPTER 1

THE VALLEY AND ITS SETTLEMENTS

The vale of Darley is situated in the Derbyshire Derwent Valley commencing approximately half a mile north of Matlock town centre to the road bridge over the River Derwent at Rowsley. Darley is bisected by the main A6 London to Carlisle trunk road and the River Derwent. The western side of our valley from Darley Bridge to the convergence of the rivers Wye and Derwent at Rowsley is very sparsely populated and well wooded and is a haven for wild life.

Population taken from Census records.

Census	South Darley	North Darley
1801	620	1,077
1811	617	990
1821	665	1,175
1831	671	1,266
1861	582	1,574
1871	605	1,557
1881	679	1,848
1891	754	2,179
1901	788	2,756
1911	809	3,317
1921	740	3,264
1931	731	4,093

1951	862	5,672	
1961	685	5,289	
1971	748	5,314	
1981	741	5,274	(with Little
1991	752	5,440	Rowsley and
1999	790	5,820	Northwood)

At the beginning of the third millennium the combined population of the Darley district exceeded six thousand. The valley is now divided into four main areas of administration, Darley Dale, South Darley, Northwood and Tinkersley, and Little Rowsley. The north east slopes of the valley are gritstone. The valley bottom is substantially flat meadow land on both sides of the river with a shale underlay. The south west slopes are mainly limestone with gritstone caps. The north east slopes and caps are gritstone. To the south west side of the Derwent, and very prominent, stands a huge mound of shale named Oker Hill, some 193 metres above sea level. This is a glacial deposit.

People have lived in the area since the dawn of history. The area has experienced in some measure most of the racial migrations which have taken place in our history. Both sides of the valley at high levels display evidence of early man's occupation, with a profusion of burial mounds and stone circles. To the east of the parish, at Winster, passes the ancient trackway dating from prehistoric times and known as the Portway. This trackway was part of a system connecting the north and south of England. There are numerous stone circles adjacent to this trackway dating back to the Bronze Age. Remnants of migrating races, such as Iberians, Celts, Romans, Saxons and Viking cultures are to be found in the area. These were followed by the Norman dynasty who ruled our valley for around six hundred years from 1066.

During the reign of Edward the Elder (son of Alfred the Great and conqueror of the Vikings), from 899 to 924, Darley Church was founded on the east side of the Derwent, astride the Old Road which led to the ford over the river Derwent at a place now named Darley Bridge.

When the Normans came to Darley Dale it was recorded in the

Domesday Book that Dereleie (deer clearing) had a priest and a church, 12 acres (4.88 hectares) of meadow, woodland pasture 2 leagues long and 2 leagues wide. "League" is from the Celtic and one league equals approximately three miles (4.828 km). Dereleie was valued at forty shillings and two sesters of honey. In the words of the Domesday Book "In Darley the King had two carucates (about 120 acres, or 50 hectares) of land taxable. In Farley, Cotes and Burley one carucate of land and two bovates (a bovate was about 16 acres) taxable, and Land for three ploughs. The King had one plough and seven villagers had three ploughs".

Darley became known in the 1800s as Darleys in the Dale because of its size and make up of scattered hamlets on the east and west sides of the valley. On the west side of the valley lie Wensley and Snitterton comprising about six thousand acres, 9½ square miles, approximately 2461 hectares. The 1801 census returned 1077 in Darley Township, and 620 in Wensley and Snitterton, a total of 1697. The 1999 combined population, including the new 1980 parish of Northwood and Tinkersley, totalled 6610. In the 1840s South Darley became a separate Parish.

The principal settlements of the Darley Dale area, starting at the north end of the Parish adjoining Great Rowsley, and going clockwise, consisted of Little Rowsley (1), Tinkersley (Cotes in Domesday Book) and Northwood (2), Darley Hillside and Burley (Berleie in the Domesday Book) (3), Central Darley and Churchtown (4), Two Dales (5), Darley Flash, Farley, Hackney, Darley House Estate, and Hooleys Estate area (6). Passing over the River Derwent about half a mile from Matlock town centre at the iron railway bridge over the Derwent, to the West side of the valley, we have the hamlets of Snitterton (7), Oker, Cross Green, Wensley (8), Darley Bridge and Cowley (9).

The numbers refer to the maps. In the 1930s there were two railway stations, five post offices, three churches and eleven chapels, all within the original Darley ecclesiastical parish.

11

FLORA AND FAUNA

Darley Dale has a heather named after it – Erica Darleyensis, a hybrid propagated in James Smith & Sons' nurseries. Sir Joseph Whitworth had a rhodedendron named after him which has crimson coloured flowers and can still be found in the area. There is a yew tree in St Helen's churchyard thought to be 2000 years old. Rabbits, badgers and foxes abound in the area. Rabbits have never been as numerous as they were before the spread of myxamatosis in the 1950s. The Barn Owl has become scarce but other owl species are plentiful. There are many woodland birds in the area and recently buzzards have been noted. Up to the second world war the native red squirrels lived in the Darley valley but after the war the American grey squirrel took over and red squirrels are no longer seen. Otters lived in the valley until the 1950s, since when there has been no sign of them except for a single sighting in 1999. Curlews have become scarce since the 1950s.

In 1944 a landowner in an adjacent valley turned his herd of over forty deer out of his deer park under orders from the wartime Agricultural Committee to enable crops to be grown there. The descendants of this herd still live in groups in the more isolated parts of our valley. After fifty-five years of suffering abuse from poachers, dogs and people pressure they have become very wary animals and are rarely seen as they have learned to stay mostly in very private areas. In bad winters they are looked after and fed by the original owners and others. The herd suffered bad losses in the severe winters of the early sixties but are now back to their original strength, over forty.

Photographs of the valley taken at the turn of the twentieth century show a valley with far fewer trees than exist today. The former Cherry Tree Farm, Darley Hillside, is now planted with woodland; the Hall Dale and Tinkersley Woods have grown to maturity, and the western slopes of the valley have become well sprinkled with thorn scrub. The wide verges of the side roads were formerly kept clear of trees, especially those used for driving cattle to market, up to the 1950s. This also helped to keep the road surface free of leaves and frost. Today many of our roadside verges and roadside walls are deteriorating fast under a plethora of self-set trees, mostly sycamores. The main reason for this is the disappearance of the "road men". Road men employed by local authorities were allotted certain lengths of highway to keep clean and tidy, and report on its state of repair. They also filled a role in society as neighbourhood watch men, guide, information officer, footpaths officer and social worker.

One of Darley Dale's roadmen became briefly famous as one of the few seemingly genuine examples of spontaneous combustion. Spontaneous human combustion is a lethal and fortunately a very rare phenomenon, occuring when a person bursts into flame for no apparent reason. Occasional cases have been reported but have never been explained. Two cases have allegedly occurred in the last century, both in America – a Mrs. Mary Reeser of St. Petersburg, Florida, in July 1951, and Dr. John Irving Bentley of Cloudersport, Pennsylvania in December 1966. Neither of these cases was witnessed.

Passers-by in Darley Dale actually witnessed a man catch fire for no apparent reason as he walked up Crowstones Road, Darley Dale, close to the junction with the A6. It was a day never to be forgotten by the people involved, especially the man who experienced this unique happening Mr. William (Bill) Salt, ex-railwayman, construction

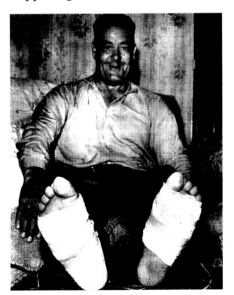

worker, and in 1963 a member of that now defunct profession, a road man. At the north end of his section Bill Salt had the use of an old stone barn, next to the railway crossing at Churchtown, Darley Dale, where he kept all his tools, wheelbarrow, brushes, weed-killer and working clothes. At the south end of his section Bill had the use of a lock up cupboard at Station Road, Darley Dale, where he kept a spare pair of shoes, a coat and a sack of weed-killer.

13

It was a lovely day as Bill swept and tidied his way along the Oaker Avenue Estate, which happened to be his section for that day, exchanging pleasantries with people en route. As he walked up Crowstones Road with his wheelbarrow Bill felt a sharp pain around his ankles. Looking down he was amazed to see he was on fire. Flames were coming from around his ankles and the conflagration quickly spread up his trousers. Bill threw himself to the ground, shouting for help, his shoes and trousers blazing. Bill, snatching off his burning shoes, was terrified, having no idea why he had set alight. He had not been near a fire or anything combustible such as petrol or creosote that day. Fortunately Bill was not in one of the more remote places on his round. Several people came to his aid, and others phoned the emergency services. Everyone was absolutely amazed and shocked at the unbelievable happening. A passing van stopped and whisked Bill off to the Whitworth Hospital, and after emergency treatment he was transferred to Derby Infirmary. At the time a local newspaper photographer took a picture of Bill's burnt and bandaged feet and ankles. When the news broke about Bill's apparently spontaneous combustion, it took the world's press by storm. Pictures of Bill and his feet were shown in newspapers world-wide.

A few days later, after investigation, the cause of Bill's apparent spontaneous combustion was solved. It was definitely spontaneous combustion, not of Bill but of his shoes. Bill had been in the habit of keeping his working shoes below the shelf where the Sodium Chlorate weed-killer was kept. At times the shoes received an accidental dusting of the weed-killer. Over a long period the shoes absorbed the Sodium Chlorate and became a fire-bomb waiting to explode, which is what duly happened. This was caused by friction between the shoes and the road surface. Bill still has a souvenir of his experience in the form of a letter from America simply addressed to "The Man whose feet caught fire, England" which was promptly delivered to Bill by Britain's excellent postal service. Bill Salt, now 92 still lives in Broad Walk, Darley Dale and says he will never forget the day when for no apparent reason he burst into flames.

LOCAL COUNCIL FORMATIONS, INVESTMENTS AND AMALGAMATIONS.

County boundaries in Britain up to 1974 had stayed roughly the same from antiquity. William the Conqueror retained and used the county shire administration that was in existence on his arrival. It is pleasing to note that in the 1990s traditional shires and county names, and approximate boundaries, were returning. All people have a pride and sense of belonging to their own traditional area; history has undoubtedly proved this.

County Councils, including Derbyshire County Council, came into being by reason of the Local Government Act of 1888, which called them into existence on 1st April (All Fools Day) 1889. In 1890 they became responsible for pauper lunatics, and in 1902 responsible for education. Since then their responsibilities have increased immensely. The first County rate levied in 1889 was a miserly 6d, or 2½p; in 1939 8/7d or 43p; in 1989 £2.17.10d or £2.89p. In 1894 Parish and District Councils were created. They were responsible for sanitation and overseers of the poor. All types of local councils through elections gave local people representation.

The ecclesiastical parish of South Darley was created on 20th August 1845. The civil parish was governed by a local Board from 1863 until 1894 when it became an Urban District Council. Joseph Potter was "Inspector of Nuisances". In 1934 it was absorbed into the Matlock Urban District Council and in 1974 became part of Derbyshire Dales District Council. Rates levied in 1934, before amalgamation with Matlock U.D.C. were ten shillings (50p) compared with Matlock's thirteen shillings (65p) and Wirksworth's five shillings and fourpence (27p) rates of 1933. In the same year, 1933, South Darley U.D.C. expressed concern over the excessive number of privy middens in Darley Bridge and Wensley, but noted that there were now no dwellings without a water supply within one hundred yards (91.44 metres).

North Darley also had a Board of Governors from 1863 to 1894 when it became North Darley U.D.C. until 1934, when, along with South Darley U.D.C., it was amalgamated into Matlock U.D.C. In 1974

West Derbyshire District Council, later Derbyshire Dales District Council, came into being by an amalgamation of the U.D.C.s. Darley Dale Parish Council, later Town Council, was created in 1980. The same year saw the creation of parish councils for South Darley, Northwood and Tinkersley.

Before 1863 the Register of persons eligible to vote for a Member of Parliament was signed by a group of people who were entitled, Church Wardens, and overseers of the Parish of Darley and Lordship of Little Rowsley.

The 1832 Reform Act gave the vote to men who were freeholders of property which was worth forty shillings a year, or those with land worth ten pounds annually, or who were leasing fifty pounds of property.

A tower on the western crest of the valley above and to the west of the hamlet of Stanton Lees was constructed to commenorate the Act. It is a prominent landmark above the valley.

COPY of such part of the Register of Persons entitled to Vote at any Election for a Member or Members to serve in Parliament for the NORTHERN DIVISION of the County of Derby, between the 30th of November, 1856, and the 1st o December, 1857, as far as relate to the Parish or Township of

DARLEY.

PARISH OR TOWNSHIP OF DARLEY—*Continued.*

Margin for Overseers' Objections.	Number.	Christian Name and Surname of each Voter at full length.	Place of Abode.	Nature of Qualification.	Street, Lane, or other like place in this Parish [or Township], and Number of House (if any) where the Property is situate, or Name of the Property, if known by any, or Name of the occupying Tenant; or if the Qualification consist of a Rent charge, then the Name of the Owners of the Property out of which such Rent is issuing, or some of them, and the Situation of the Property.
	783	Broomhead, Benjamin	Hackney lane, near Matlock Bath	Freehold house and land	Hackney lane
	784	Bowring, Arundel	Hackney lane, near Matlock Bath	House and land as occupier	Hackney lane
	785	Bowman, Richard Lomax	Darley hill side	Freehold land and buildings	John Willis and others
	786	Bowler, John	Hackney lane, Darley	Freehold house and land	Hackney lane
	787	Cramind, William	Belper	Freehold house and land	Hackney lane
	788	Cowley, John	Toadhole, near Matlock Bath	Freehold house and land	Toadhole
	789	Crew, Lewis Edmund	Repton park, Derbyshire	Freehold houses	Hackney lane
	790	Clarke, Charles, Esq.	Matlock Bath	Freehold house and land	Upper Hackney
	791	Clayton, Robert	Darley bridge	Freehold houses	Darley Bridge
	792	Davis, William	Matlock bank	Freehold land	Darley hill side
	793	Dakeyne, Charles	Toadhole, near Matlock	Freehold land	Toadhole moor
	794	Dakeyne, Baldwin	Toadhole, near Matlock	Freehold land	Toadhole moor
	795	Derbyshire, Jonathan	Toadhole, near Matlock Bath	Freehold house and land	Own occupation
	796	Dakeyne, James	Toadhole, near Matlock Bath	Freehold house and land	Toadhole
	797	Dakeyne, Edward	Toadhole, near Matlock Bath	Freehold land	Nab side
	798	Derbyshire Joseph	Wensley, near Matlock Bath	Freehold house and land	Darley hill side
	799	Derbyshire, John	Toadhole, near Matlock Bath	Freehold house and land	Toadhole ; in my own occupation
	800	Derbyshire, John	Darley moor, near Matlock Bath	Freehold house and land	Darley hill side
	801	Dunn, John	Upper Hackney, near Matlock Bath	House and land as occupier	Upper Hackney
Ejected	802	Derbyshire, John	Toadhole, near Matlock Bath	Land, house, and buildings as occupier	Toadhole
	803	Derbyshire, Francis	Stonegravels, Chesterfield	Freehold house and land	Toadhole
	804	Derbyshire, Henry	Darley moor, near Matlock Bath	Freehold land	Darley hill side
	805	Else, John	Matlock	Freehold land	Hackney lane
	806	Else, John	Darley mill	Occupation of house, mill, and land	Darley mill
	807	Evans, John	Alport, Bakewell	Occupation of house and land	Northwood, Darley
	808	Evans, Thomas	Northwood, near Matlock Bath	Land and buildings as occupier	Darley
	809	Foster, Henry	Scale lane, Hull	Freehold house and land	Farley
	810	Fielding, Henry	Hackney lane, near Matlock Bath	Rent charge on freehold land	Darley Abbey ; James Fielding, owner
	811	Fielding, John	Butts, Darley, near Matlock Bath	Rent charge on freehold land	Darley Abbey ; James Fielding, owner
	812	Garton, John	Lumsdale, Matlock	Freehold land	Hackney lane
	813	Grafton, Samuel	Beeley	Freehold land	Darley ; own occupation
	814	Guite, Samuel	Darley hill side	Freehold land	Darley hill side

PARISH OR TOWNSHIP OF DARLEY—*Continued.*

Margin for Overseers' Objections.	Number.	Christian Name and Surname of each Voter at full length.	Place of Abode.	Nature of Qualification.	Street, Lane, or other like place in this Parish [or Township], and Number of House (if any) where the Property is situate, or Name of the Property, if known by any, or Name of the occupying Tenant; or if the Qualification consist of a Rent-charge, then the Name of the Owner of the Property out of which such Rent is issuing, or some of them, and the Situation of the Property.
	815	Gregory, Benjamin	Hackney lane, near Matlock Bath	House and land as occupier	Hackney lane
	816	Gregory, George	Darley hill side, near Matlock Bath	Freehold house and land	Northwood
	817	Gill, John	Darley hill side, near Matlock Bath	Freehold house and land	Darley hill side
	818	Holmes, Samuel	Darley hill side, near Matlock Bath	Freehold house and land	Darley hill side ; William Rawson
	819	Holmes, Anthony	Darley bridge, Wensley, near Matlock Bath	Freehold land	Darley Bridge
	820	Harrison, Thomas	Belper	Freehold houses	Hackney lane
	821	Holmes, Samuel	Tor side, Darley	Freehold house and land	Tor side, Darley
	822	Hall, John Wall	Darley hill side	Freehold land	Darley hill side
	823	Harrison, John	Belper	Freehold houses	Hackney lane
	824	Harrison, James	Belper	Freehold houses	Hackney lane
	825	Holland, Thomas	Tinkersley, near Matlock Bath	Freehold house and land	Darley hill side
	826	Ibbotson, Thomas	Broomfield, Glossop road, Sheffield	Freehold houses and land	Francis White and others
	827	Jebb, Samuel Henry	Boston	Freehold estate	Wood-at-Flash
	828	Jebb, Joshua	7, Summers' place, London	Freehold estate	Moor Hall
	829	Kinnersley, Joseph	Upper Hackney, near Matlock Bath	Freehold house and land	Upper Hackney
Ejected, Dead	830	King, James	Upper Hackney, near Matlock Bath	Freehold house and land	Upper Hackney
	831	Leacroft, William Swymer	Southwell	Share of freehold land, and mill	James Dakeyne
	832	Leeys, Henry	Northwood	Land, house, and buildings as occupier	Northwood
	833	Milner, John	Edensor, near Bakewell	Freehold house and land	Darley hill side
	834	Mitchel, Sampson	Nab, Darley, near Matlock Bath	Freehold house and land	Nab
	835	Manson, Robert Frederick	11, Down street, Piccadilly, London	Freehold rent charge	Darley dale ; Mrs Ann Manson
	836	Milner, Henry	Chatsworth, near Bakewell	Freehold house and land	Darley hill side ; Samuel Wrigg
	837	Milward, James	Darley hill side, near Matlock Bath	Freehold house and land	Toadhole
Dead,	838	Manson, Alexander Thomas Grist	Beeston, Notts	Freehold rent charge	Mrs. Ann Manson, Darley
	839	Millward, George	Upper Hackney, near Matlock Bath	Freehold house and land	Upper Hackney
	840	Milward, John	Upper Hackney, near Matlock Bath	Freehold house and land	Upper Hackney
	841	Manson, William Pitt	45, Duncan Terrace, Islington, London	Freehold rent charge	Mrs. Ann Manson, Darley Dale
	842	Nuttall, Samuel	Churchtown, Darley, near Matlock Bath	House and land as occupier	Church town

18

Margin or Overseers' Objections.	Number.	Christian Name and Surname of each Voter at full length.	Place of Abode.	Nature of Qualification.	Street, Lane, or other like place in this Parish [or Township], and Number of House (if any) where the Property is situate, or Name of the Property, if known by any, or Name of the occupying Tenant; or if the Qualification consist of a Rent-charge, then the Names of the Owners of the Property out of which such Rent is issuing, or some of them, and the Situation of the Property.
	843	Pilkington, William	Toadhole, near Matlock Bath	Freehold house, land, and garden	Toadhole
	844	Parks, Henry	Northwood, Darley, near Matlock Bath	Freehold house and land	Northwood
	845	Parks, John	Upper Hackney, near Matlock Bath	House and land as occupier	Upper Hackney
	846	Smith, John	Norton, near Sheffield	Freehold houses and land	Darley dale
	847	Smith, Samuel	Combe Hurst, near Kingston-on-Thames, Surrey	Freehold land	Darley hill side
	848	Smith, Thomas	Farley, Darley, near Matlock Bath	Freehold house and land	Farley ; own occupation
	849	Stevens, Henry	Matlock	Freehold house and land	Darley hill side
	850	Stevens, Edward	Farley	House and land as occupier	Farley
	851	Smith, George	Aldern house, Bakewell	Freehold land	Stock house ; William Preston
	852	Tomlinson, John	Lordship, Darley, near Matlock Bath	House and land as occupier	Little Rowsley
	853	Taylor, Henry	Toadhole, near Matlock Bath	Freehold land	Nab
	854	Vains, John	Upper Hackney, near Matlock Bath	Freehold house and land	Upper Hackney
	855	Vawdrey, Daniel	Darley rectory	Freehold house and land	The rectory
	856	Wildgoose, Thomas	No. 87 and 89, Mill Street, Macclesfield, Cheshire	Undivided share of freehold land and buildings	Lawrances Wildgoose and Francis Wildgoose
	857	Wilmot, Thomas	Ripley	Freehold house and land	Thomas Wildgoose
	858	Wildgoose, Anthony	Hackney lane, near Matlock Bath	Freehold land	Farley
	859	Wall, John	Fallinge, Darley, near Matlock Bath	House and land as occupier	Fallinge
	860	Wooller, John	Beeston, Notts.	Freehold house and land	Farley
	861	Wildgoose, Francis	Hurst, near Matlock Bath	Share of freehold houses and land	Thomas Wildgoose & others
	862	Wildgoose, Lawrence	Hurst, near Matlock Bath	Share of freehold houses and land	Thomas Wildgoose & others
	863	Wilmot, John	Darley hill side, near Matlock Bath	Freehold house and land	Darley hill side
	864	Wilson, Richard	Bumper castle, Darley, near Matlock Bath	House and land as occupier	Bumper Castle
	865	Wall, George	Tor side, Darley, near Matlock Bath	Freehold houses and land	Butts
	866	Waterfall, William	Toadhole, near Matlock	Freehold land	Nab field ; own occupation
	867	Wildgoose, Richard	Darley hill side, near Matlock Bath	Freehold house and land	Darley hill side
	868	Wells, William	Belper	Freehold house and land	Hackney lane
	869	Washington, Adam	Darley house	House and land as occupier	Darley house
	870	Wayne, William Henry	Much Wenlock, Shropshire	Freehold house and land	Darley moor ; John Derbyshire
	871	Young, Charles	Matlock	Freehold land	Upper Hackney, Darley ; Joseph King
	872	Young, John	Hackney lane, near Matlock Bath	Freehold house and land	Darley hill side

John Derbyshire } Churchwardens

Walter Gorley } and

John Else } Overseers of the Parish

John Bowler } of Darley & Lea

of Little Rows

Assistant Overs

KEY TO VARIOUS AREAS

Housing

1.1 Rowsley housing

2.1 Deeleys Row

2.2 Dungreave Avenue

2.3 Park Terrace

2.4 Northwood Lane

4.1 Green Lane

4.2 The Triangle

4.4 South Park Estate

5.1 Station Road

6.1 Darley House Estate

6.2 Holt Lane

6.3 Hooleys Estate

8.5 Eversleigh Rise

Historic

3.1 Site of second Darley Hall

7.3 Bull Ring

3.2 Third Darley Hall (existing)

8.1 The Green

4.3 Site of first Darley Hall

Notable buildings

3.3 Stancliffe Hall

3.4 Stancliffe Gardens

3.5 Springfield

3.6 Orchard House

3.7 Oak Cottage

3.8 Wingate

3.9 Whitworth Laundry

4.3 Abbey House

4.7 Whitworth Centre

5.2 Wheatley House

5.3 National School

5.4 Reading Room

5.5 Chapel

5.6 Blacksmiths

5.7/8/9 Dakeyne Houses

5.10 Holt House

5.11 Flax Mill

5.12 Knabb Hall

5.13 Sydnope Hall

6.4 St. Elphins

6.5 Normanhurst

6.6 Darley House

6.7 Whitworth Hospital

7.1 Snitterton Hall

7.2 Snitterton Manor House

8.2 Old Reading Room

8.3 New Reading Room

8.4 Village Hall

8.6 Wensley Hall

9.1 Cowley

9.2 Stanton Stand

Roads

2.4 Signpost	2.7 Abandoned Road
2.5 Old High route	3.10 Hall Dale Lane
2.6 Old Low route	4.5 Signpost
2.7 Abandoned road	5.14 Signpost

Darley boundaries

1.2 Old Boundary	6.8 Darley/Matlock Boundary

Railways

1.3 Paxton's Station	5.15 Darley Sidings
1.4 Rowsley Sidings	4.6 Abandoned Stancliffe Railway

The principal settlements of the Darley Dale area, starting at the north end of the Parish adjoining Great Rowsley, and going clockwise, consisted of Little Rowsley (1), Tinkersley (Cotes in Domesday Book) and Northwood (2), Darley Hillside and Burley (Berleie in the Domesday Book) (3), Central Darley and Churchtown (4), Two Dales (5), Darley Flash, Farley, Hackney, Darley House Estate, and Hooleys Estate area (6). Passing over the River Derwent about half a mile from Matlock town centre at the iron railway bridge over the Derwent, to the West side of the valley, we have the hamlets of Snitterton (7), Oker, Cross Green, Wensley (8), Darley Bridge and Cowley (9).

The numbers refer to the maps. Principal settlements are numbered to match those on Maps.

The Map of Darley Dale is in four sections, A, B, C and D. The location numbers coincide with the Hamlet numbers.

HOUSING

In the medieval period dwellings were inclined to cluster around manor houses, churches and farmsteads. Darley east and west of the Derwent occupied such a vast area, almost from Matlock to Beeley and from Darley Flash to near the Winster and Tearsall area, that inevitably a series of small hamlets developed. As one local historian pointed out,

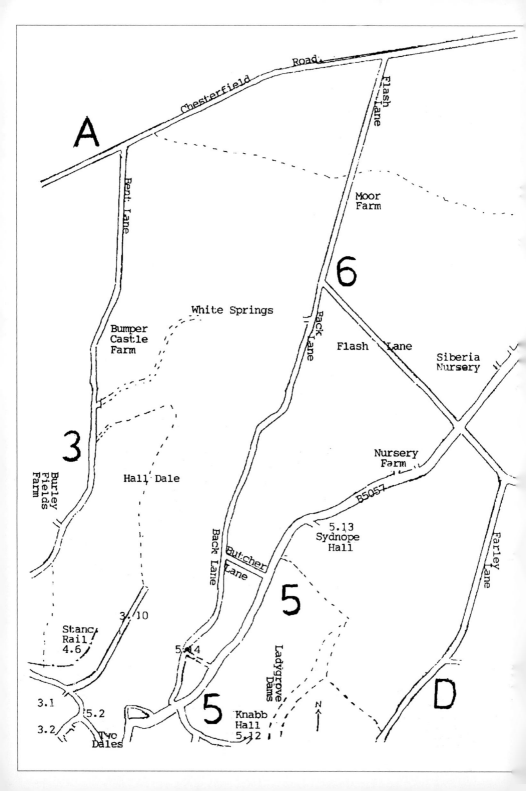

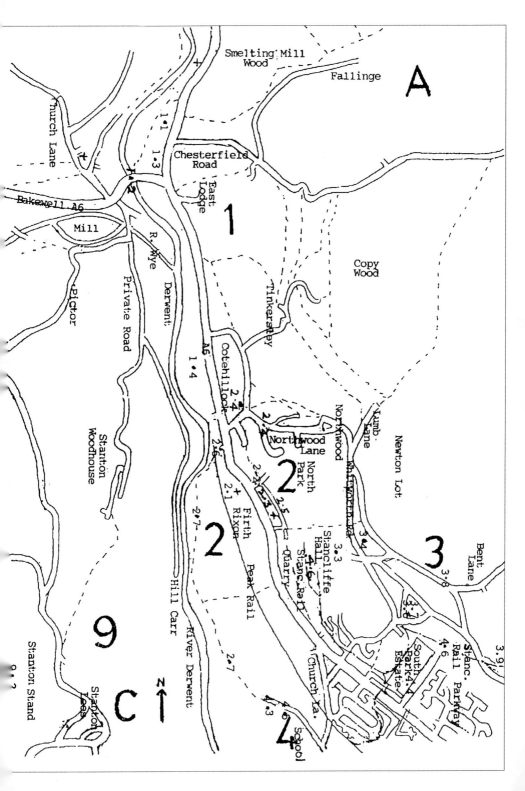

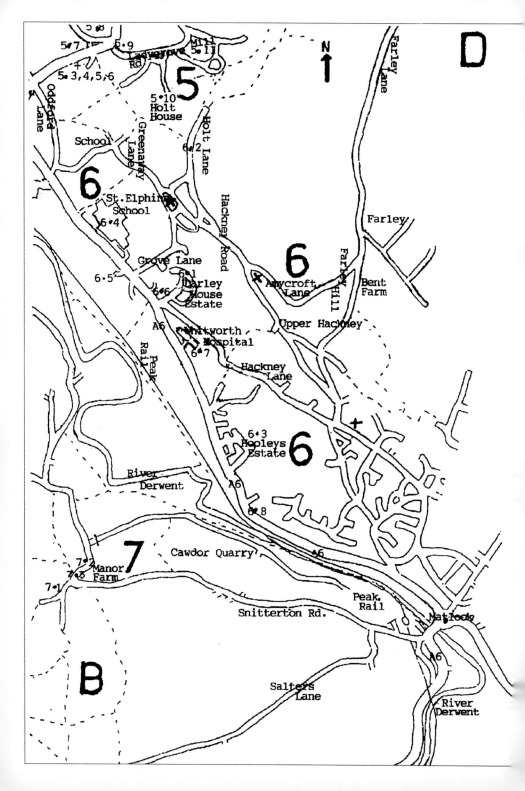

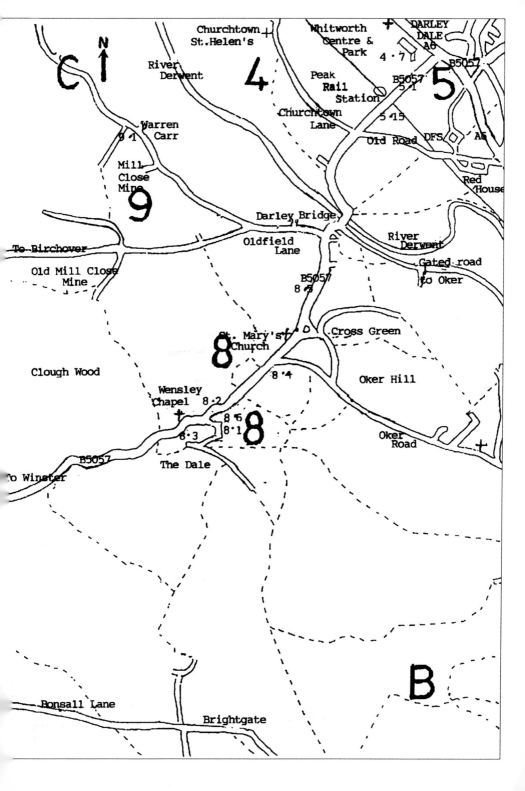

the centre of Darley, Churchtown, was a church without a town. In the 1880s the land adjacent to the A6 from Northwood Lane to the Matlock boundary began to be developed and is now the main residential area.

The Darley and district population has shown a steady upward growth from the first Census in 1801 to the present day. Growth was particularly fast between the 1891 census, when the population was 2,933 and that taken in 1951, when the figure was 6534. The combined population of Darley Dale, Northwood and South Darley was 6,610 in 1999.

The railway company constructed housing at Little Rowsley in 1871 for their workers. The area near the bottom of Northwood Lane expanded southwards at the same time. Some of these houses, including Deeleys Row, are now demolished. The houses at Dungreave Avenue and Park Terrace were constructed around this time, and also housing at Ryecroft and Park Lane, Two Dales. Two Dales was the largest settlement at the beginning of the twentieth century.

On the south side of Green Lane/Church Road area was the housing constructed by Sir Joseph Whitworth in the 1870s for his estate workers. In the early part of the twentieth century these houses were known as Canon Row because of the finial, i.e. the highest point of the gable, which was modelled on the Whitworth artillery shell fired from his hexagonal-barrelled field gun. The north side of Green Lane/Church Road triangle was built around 1910 to house the rapidly expanding Stancliffe work force. There were six shops for these two groups of housing. Housing was built down Station Road before the First World War by Robert Lehane, builder, quarry owner and future joint founder of the civil engineering firm Lehane Mackenzie & Shand. Twyfords from Two Dales built various houses around Darley and South Darley until the mid thirties, when they ceased trading. Twyford's house and yard were next to the National School at Two Dales.

The pre-First World War surge in house building resulted in extensions to the Darley and South Darley Church of England schools and the building of a completely new school at Greenaway Lane, in 1912.

During and after the 1914 War house building remained quiet until the mid 1920s when a builder called Charles Wildgoose, who lived at Darley House, built what we would call today speculative housing, at Darley House estate, Holt Road, Central Darley and Darley Hillside. His dwellings included a large proportion of bungalows.

Stancliffe Estate, successors of Sir Joseph Whitworth, were still the largest landowners in Darley up to 1947, the time of their demise. Among their holdings was the area between Northwood Lane and Park Lane at Two Dales. The area from Northwood Lane to Stancliffe Hall grounds was called North Park, and the area from Stancliffe Hall grounds southwards to Park Lane, Two Dales, was called South Park. A builder from Manchester, Mr. Morton, became Managing Director of Stancliffe Estates, just after the turn of the twentieth century and in 1923 he commenced building the large South Park Estate, now better known as Broad Walk. Morton built over one hundred and fifty houses and eight shops. The estate commenced with a shop next to the Grouse Inn on the A6. The Green Lane housing already had six shops including a Post Office. Six shops were built of precast stone on the A6 south of Broad Walk, and also three pairs of quality houses known as The Villas which were finished around 1935, thereby completing the estate. Most of the Broad Walk estate was built by three bricklaying brothers, Harry, Tommy and Bob Ainscough, who, along with their labourer, Jack Roberts, all from Manchester, became a legend in the construction industry. Harry was always known, though not to his face, as Mad Harry because of his work rate. Bob was still alive in 2000 and living at Darley Bridge.

The 1930s also saw the building of Hooley's Estate on the A6 just north of the Matlock/Darley boundary, containing approximately 190 dwellings and one shop. The two bricklaying brothers Kemp were the main builders.

Prior to the First World War there were no dwellings on Northwood Lane from the A6 up to the old stone-built settlement near the top, which has dwellings dated back to the 1600s clustered around a triangular open space and a water trough, still there. Through the 20s and 30s ribbon development took place on both sides of Northwood Lane from the A6 to fifty metres short of its junction on with Lumb Lane, mostly built by Ezra Toft's bullding firm.

South Darley also suffered ribbon development in the 1920-30 period. Eversleigh Rise was built by Twyfords in the mid-30s. St. Mary's View and the Oker Lane houses opposite were also built in the 1930s, the latter by George Fidler. Wensley also acquired new housing, thanks to a local benefactor, Mr. Joseph Taylor.

By 1939 Darley had changed in fifty years from the old mostly local agriculture-based group of settlements to new industrial and commuter based ones. In 1889 there were practically no workers' dwellings on the A6 through Darley Dale between Little Rowsley and the Darley/Matlock boundary. Over the last fifty years housing developments in the Darley valley have grown at a great pace, including local authority housing with the Crowstones Road/Oaker Avenue estate, Park Lane, Two Dales, Underhall complex and Gold Close at South Darley. Various builders, including Matlock builders John William Wildgoose and Sons, have completely covered the remaining area of South Park, south east of Broad Walk, with private dwellings. Sixty private dwellings have been built in the area around the Stancliffe Works since 1965, approximately forty of them by Lewis Jackson Builders. Loscoe Row and Deeley's Row have been demolished since 1950.

In 1999 plans were passed to build over two hundred dwellings between Hackney Lane and the Hooley Estate area. These, coupled with the construction between 1970 and 1990 of houses on the Stanton Moor View estate, will see a substantial settlement of about five hundred dwellings on the east of the A6 between the Whitworth Hospital and the Darley/Matlock boundary. Prior to the 1920s there were only four dwellings in that area, two on Hackney Lane and two near to the rear of the Whitworth Hospital. Upper Hackney, built along the spring line on the sunny south facing slopes, is a classic example of building housing in a good location with good water, views, shelter from the north east weather. Hackney is a linear settlement almost a mile long, with no industrial base. Darley House Estate is an example of 1920-30s isolated speculative housing, which again has no industrial base.

Smedley Street East. Boundary of Darley Dale until 1980s when it was moved 200 metres west so that the new All Saints School could be in Matlock

Rowsley Bridge from the south.
Entering Darley Dale from the north, the boundary stone is on the right and the widening date stone is on the left.

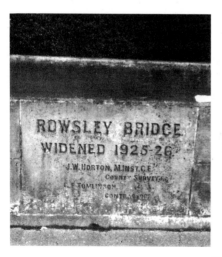

This Agreement made this *Fourth* day of *April* One thousand *eight hundred ninety nine* BETWEEN THE TRUSTEES OF THE WHITWORTH INSTITUTE Darley Dale hereinafter called the Landlords by JOSEPH HENRY DAWSON of Darley Dale in the County of Derby their Secretary and Agent of the one part and *Herbert Wragg* of *Upper Hackney* Darley Dale aforesaid hereinafter called the Tenant of the other part **Whereby** the Landlords agree to let and the Tenant agrees to hire the Allotment numbered *44* on the plan of Allotments hereto annexed and thereon coloured red at the yearly rent of *7/6ᵈ* subject to the following conditions—

1. The Allotment is let and taken for one year and the tenancy shall date from the first day of January in each year.

2. The rent shall be paid in one sum annually on the first day of July in each year. If unpaid at the expiration of fourteen days from that date it shall be recoverable in like manner as in any other case of Landlord and Tenant.

3. The Tenancy may be determined by either party by giving to the other three months notice in writing expiring on the first day of January next after such notice has been given.

4. The Tenant shall not erect on the Allotment any building or shed except a wooden toolhouse and an arbour or either of them and shall always keep such erections in good and neat order and condition.

5. The Tenant shall not sublet nor transfer his holding to any other person nor employ any third person to work the Allotment without the written consent of the Landlords or their Agent and without full explanation of the conditions and consideration of such arrangement.

6. The Allotment shall be used for a Garden Plot only. No Tenant may keep a pig or pigs in his Allotment.

7. The Landlords will pay all rates taxes and tithes which may become due and payable on each Allotment.

As Witness the hands of the said parties the day and year first above written.

Signed by the said JOSEPH HENRY DAWSON
and the said *Herbert Wall*

in the presence of
Herbert Wall
Darley Dale

J H Dawson
Herbert Wragg

31

GARDEN ALLOTMENTS IN THE UPPER MIDDLE
DARLE
AS ARRANGED FEB. I

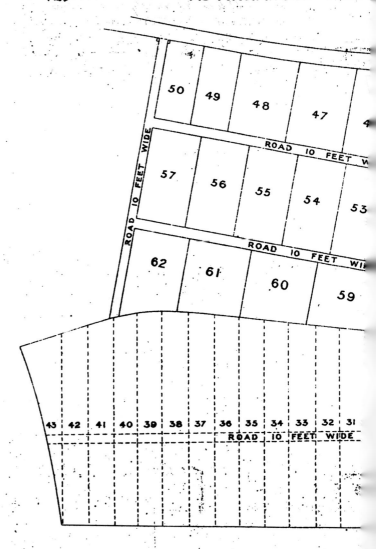

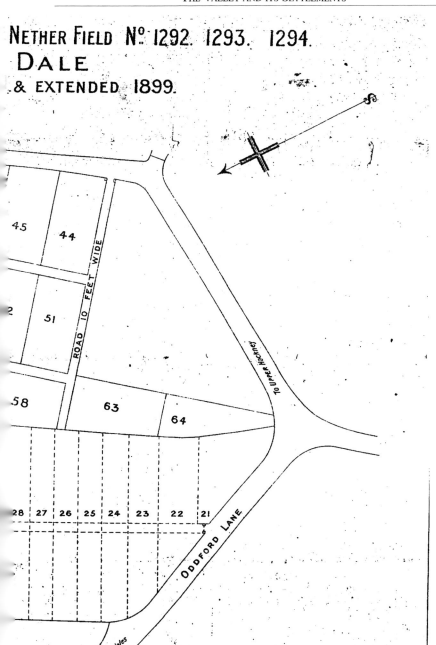

NETHER FIELD N.º 1292. 1293. 1294.
DALE
& EXTENDED 1899.

45 44

ROAD 10 FEET WIDE

2 51

10 UPPER Hockney

58 63

64

28 | 27 | 26 | 25 | 24 | 23 | 22 | 21

ODDFORD LANE

Two-dales

Greenaway School. Built 1913 on the site of the Whitworth Garden Allotments of 1895 purchased from the Whitworth Trustees

Church Town School, early 1900s

Church Town School, early 1900s

Whitworth Institute as a hospital during the First World War

FROM THE NORTH DARLEY URBAN DISTRICT COUNCIL.

As the representatives of this parish, we wish to convey to you our sincere congratulations on the victorious conclusion of War.

We have read and heard from time to time during the past four years of the splendid achievements of our Darley lads and we are proud of you all. You have helped to make it possible for mankind to live in security, and we thank you on behalf of this parish with all the earnestness of which our grateful hearts are capable. That you may live long to enjoy the blessings of a lasting peace is the sincere wish and prayer of us all. Wishing you the compliments of the season and a prosperous future.

We remain,

Your grateful friends,

C. S. ANTHONY, *Chairman.*   W. PITTS, *Vice-Chairman.*
W. WHITE.   H. HOLMES.   S. S. WARDMAN.
J. HEWITSON.   W. WARD.   R. H. BAKER.
J. SMITH.   R. LEHANE.   F. B. WILDGOOSE.

F. C. LAMB, *Clerk.*
E. F. LOMAS, *Surveyor.*
W. R. Alston, *Collector.*

36

The War Memorial Cross 1914-18. Whitworth Institute grounds, Darley Dale
27 April 1921

A6 Dale Road in the 1900s from 300 metres south of Firth Rixson to the Whitworth
Hospital.
Elias Morton and George Holland taken opposite Homesfield, Dale Road North 1919

A6 top of Church Lane junction 1920s

A6 Church Lane. West Lodge main entrance to Sir Joseph Whitworth's Stancliffe Hall 1890s then open to the A6

A6 Church Lane 1970. Showing bungalow made of poured concrete 1920s. Concrete shuttering taken to Bakewell, re-erected at Aldern House, Peak Park headquarters, and twin bungalow cast at bottom of old drive entrance (still in situ)

Whitworth Road A6 junction 1920s

Opposite Whitworth Road A6 junction 1920s.
First shop Jim and Daisy Woolliscroft, Miss Boam papershop, Miss Siddall post office,
Mr Fielding cobbler's shop, Mr Fearn haberdashery (all on right hand side)
Stancliffe Works on the left

Grouse Inn 1900s

A6 taken from Grouse Inn 1921. Bungalow on the right was the home of Mr Anthony, Headmaster of Churchtown School

Bottom of sandy path (Peakland View) Darley Hillside 1900s

Peakland View, Darley Hillside, early 1970s (same view as previous picture)

A6 in the 1930s
On the left, butcher's shop now a dwelling, next to the Grouse Inn and Orme's provision shop. On the right the Darley Dale Derwent Valley Co-op, formerly the home of Mr Anthony, Headmaster of Churchtown School

1900s Darley Hillside from A6 where Peakland View now stands showing railway loopline to Hall Dale Quarry and the Stancliffe South Park tip, now the Darley recreation ground

Broad Walk shops 1930s

Dale Road late 1920s

Dale Road Methodist Chapel early 1900s. The tall tree on the left is an oak tree and with the one outside the Whitworth Institute was incorporated into the lime tree avenue

Whitworth Institute 1990
Note oak tree on the left and small lime trees

A6 Toplis's Garage 1937. Now Loggins and Texaco petrol station

Jim Toplis at his home Hazel House in 1985. In the National Strike of 1926, Jim drove a steam traction engine towing three trailers to Immingham Dock to fetch sugar for Ormes. It took ten days, when he got back the strike was over. Jim was a genius with engines, petrol diesel and steam

Whitworth Hospital

Yew tree and church Darley Dale

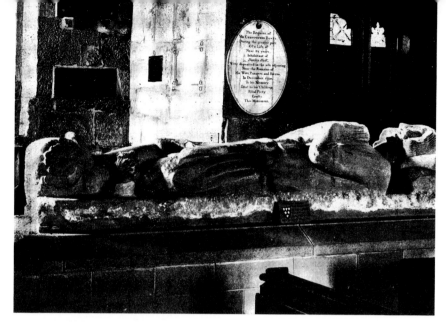

*Sir John De Darley, oldest monument in the church. In 1309 he was the governor of
Peak Castle. In 1321 John built the second Darley Hall known as Nether Hall*

St Helen's Church. Coffin lids and stone coffins

Derwent Lane leading to Nanny Goat crossing. Derwent Lane before the A6 was constructed in the 1830s was the low route to St Helen's Church and Darley Bridge abandoned as a road in the early 1900s

DARLEY TOLL HOUSE

In 1831 a specification was issued "for the building of a Toll House at the east end of the New Diversion of Road now making in Darley". The outside walls were to be of stone the same dimensions and scapeled the same as the new school at Darley, and the house was to have 12 windows, four two light ones and the remainder single light. There were to be two fireplaces, one in the "house" with boiler, oven and range, the other in the "front chamber" was to have a small range and both were to be provided at the expense of the trustees who were also to supply the cast iron window frames. On a plan of the building some stairs have been indicated and the specification includes "11 or 12 steps of stairs 2 ft 8 in long to be out of inch deal".

Joseph Watts agreed with Matthew Frost surveyor of the Third District of Nottingham to build the Toll House for the sum of one hundred and ten pounds and complete the work on or before the 8th September 1831. His signature was given on the 8th July which allowed exactly two months for doing the work.

A week previously Watts had submitted his "Tender for Getting Materials and Bulding a Toll Bar House for Darley Dale According to Plan, and with men to carry out work on the Darley Improvement, the agreements were all signed on the 19th January 1831 and the work was to be completed on or before the 15th April next. The names of the men and the prices agreed were:

Lot 1	Samuel Wragg, Jos Wragg, William Nail
Lot 2	Sam Nail
Lot 3	Francis Staley, George Carson

Cutting & Forming

Lot 1 3¹/₂d per yard.	Lot 2 8s per rood.	Lot 3 7d per yd.
	Large drains	
8¹/₂d " "	8d " yard	1s " "
	Small drains	
4d " "	3¹/₂d "	6d " "

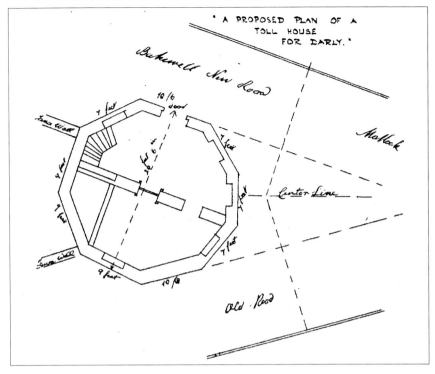

1831 Toll House at the junction of A6 and Old Road

Breast walls

1/4d " "   1/3d "   1/4d " "

Stoning the road

99s " rood   8s " rood   10/11 " "

Copies of two orders were issued in 1839 by J. Barker, Clerk to the Trustees, one headed Matlock Road and the other, sent from Burre House, (Bakewell) to Mr. Frost, surveyor, Nottingham & Newhaven or 3 District Turnpike Road.

Apr. 5. Ordered that the surveyor pay Josh Evans of Darley, miller, £1 15 0d. as compensation for diverting the water from his mill during the time the Darley road improvement was in progress.

Apr. 6. The Surveyor of Highways of the nether part of Darley having delivered a bill for £5 3s 2d. for making the footways, Mr. Frost, surveyor, was directed to inspect the same and pay towards the making such sum as he may think proper.

CHAPTER 2

HISTORY

THE DARLEYS AND COLUMBELLS

When William Duke of Normandy was preparing for his invasion of England a certain Edmond of Erle in Normandy was one of William's cavalry officers and knights. Edmond, who was born in born 1034, was granted possession of the vale of Dereleie in 1066. Sir Edmond furnished and supervised the care and handling of William's horses. William landed in England at the end of September 1066, and fought the Battle of Hastings on 14th October. November and December were spent subjugating England and dividing it among his followers whom he left with men-at-arms at strategic points to guard against uprising. William then returned to London and was crowned King on Christmas Day 1066. Edmond's wife and young son John, born at Erle in 1066, came and joined him in Darley soon afterwards. Edmond, as was the French custom, took the name Edmond de (of) Darley. He constructed himself a manor house, probably of wood, alongside the road called Derwent Lane, 220 metres north of St. Helen's Church, Darley, on or near the site of the present day Abbey House.

The present owners, whilst excavating for a swimming pool, came across what they believe to be the remains of a moat which may have surrounded the stone building that eventually replaced the wooden one. According to Glover it was a building of considerable size. It was pulled down in 1771 on the orders of the Duke of Rutland.

In 1067, whilst King William was away in Normandy, there was a rebellion in the York area, led by Edgar Atheling, the last survivor of the English royal family. William returned to England and marched north to York. Edmond de Darley and his horses went with William to York and helped to put the rebellion down. William granted lands in the area to Edmond and asked him to guard the area. Edmond and his elder son John (born 1066) took up residence at Wistow about twelve miles south of York in about 1085. Edmond's second son Richard, born at Darley in 1070, became Lord of the manor of Darley and John became Lord of the Manor of Wistow. There is another village called Darley near Harrogate, in Yorkshire.

The Yorkshire Darleys prospered. In the 15-1600s they became ship builders and merchant adventurers, building the ships that took the Pilgrim Fathers to America – the Mayflower, the Seaflower, the Abigail and the Bonaventura. Thomas Darley became an early settler in America, according to the Society of Genealogists. He was held prisoner in the American War of Independence in 1780. After the war he took up residence in South Carolina. It is also recorded that in 1624 a John Darley sailed to Virginia on the Jacob. There is no doubt that according to records several Yorkshire Darleys were early settlers in America.

The Darleys of our parish are next recorded about four generations after the Richard who was alive in 1070. William was born in 1194. William's son Andrew, born in 1215, was made Lord of the Royal Forest in the King's Peak in 1249. Andrew at that time was also Lord of Bakewell. I personally wonder if there is any connection with the inscribed stone coffin lids in St. Helen's Church porch and the Darleys. Andrew died in 1272 aged 57 and was succeeded by his son Hugh, who may have had a connection to Darley Abbey, at Derby.

The next member of the family of whom there is any real information is Sir John de Darley, great-grandson of Andrew. In 1321 Sir John engaged master masons to build him a large Manor House on the southern end of Darley Hillside, close to the old road which ran from Darley Bridge to Hall Dale Lane. This dwelling was superceded by the present Darley Hall. In 1796 the old Manor House was demolished by Richard Arkwright, who used the stone to help build his cotton mills. Arkwright built the present Darley Hall in 1790. Digressing, I think it is amazing that Richard Arkwright and Joseph Whitworth, both of humble origin, two of the men who, in my opinion, contributed immensely to the Industrial Revolution (factories and precision engineering) should have been Lords of the Manor of Darley through their ownership of Darley Hall.

Sir John de Darley died in 1350 whilst out hunting, and his eldest son Edmond (three hundred years after the first Edmond) died soon afterwards with no issue. Ralph, Sir John's second son, was the last male Darley. In 1370/71 his daughter and heiress Agnes married Thomas Columbell of Sandiacre and adopted the 1321 Nether Hall as their home. Sir Godfrey Foljambe purchased the old hall (Churchtown) in 1388.

The old estate passed through an heiress into the hands of the Plumptons, being later returned to the Columbells in the early 1500s. After passing through various hands the old hall was sold to Sir John Manners in 1631. Sir John Manners was the ancestor of the Duke of Rutland.

Peter Columbell in his will dated 20th October 1616 left his goods to his son Roger on condition that he refrained from smoking tobacco. The last of the Columbells, John, died in 1673 ending the reign of the Darley/Columbell dynasty which had lasted over six hundred years.

John Columbell's daughter and heiress took the estate to her husband, a Marbury, who died shortly afterwards, the estate reverting back to her. Now a very rich lady, she gave the lands, out of love to her husband's memory, to his relations the Thackers, who sold the estate off in parcels. Another part of the original Darley manor was held by the Kendall family.

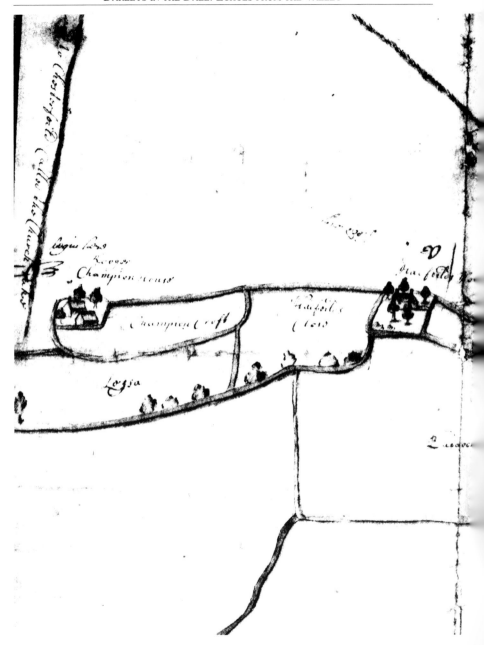

Land adjoining Nether Hall

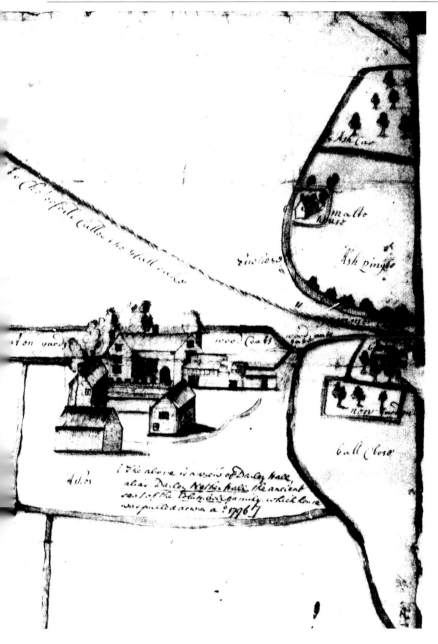

1321 Nether Hall, second seat of the Darleys

NOTABLE BUILDINGS

Stancliffe Hall was built, probably in the late 1500s, for a branch of the Columbell family, successors to the Darley and Columbell families and was passed down through successive female heirs eventually to the family of Newsam and Pott. It then became the property of Sir John Digby of Mansfield Woodhouse, who in 1655 sold it to Robert Steene of Bridgetown (Darley Bridge). In 1715 the Hall was owned by Sir Paul Jenkinson who gave it to his daughter Lettice, who in 1718 sold it to Robert Greensmith for £1750. The next owner was William Heathcote of Batavia in the colony of Demerara, who purchased the Hall and estate for £10,500 in 1799. Upon his death he bequeathed it to his brother John who died in 1821 and bequeathed it to his nephew Arthur Heathcote Heathcote who returned from Demerara to live there.

Arthur's young son Arthur died on the passage home in 1821, and another son, William in 1822, aged 7. Their sister Emily died aged 3 months in 1828, and all three are buried in St. Helen's Churchyard.

Sir Joseph Whitworth, born in Stockport in 1803, bought Stancliffe Hall in 1855 and between 1856 and his death purchased a large portion of the old manor of Darley. After the death of his wife in 1896 the estate was purchased by the company Stancliffe Estates Ltd. The Hall was then let as a school, Stancliffe Hall Preparatory School. Stancliffe Estates ceased trading in 1947 when it is believed the Hall became the property of the school's headmaster, Hugh Welch, who sold it to Mr A.K. Wareham in 1961. The school closed in 2001.

Sir Joseph's walled garden, accessed by a tunnel from the Stancliffe Hall side of Whitworth Road, was completed in the year of his death, 1887. The main Lodge there was occupied by Walter Wall, head gardener to Sir Joseph. The Wall family, as stated by Tilly in "Old Halls, Manors and Families", had been Knights of the Plough in Darley for over twenty generations, and had quietly and enduringly lived in the valley for six centuries.

Close by the walled garden, at the top of Foggs Hill, stands the house called Springfield. Foggs Hill is so called after the Misses Fogg who resided there. Springfield was purchased by the nursery family of

Stancliffe Hall 1900s

Derbyshire, who still live there in 2001.

There are several more houses of interest on Darley Hillside – Oak Cottage and Orchard House on Moor Lane, Hillcroft on Hall Moor Road, and Wingate at the junction of Bent Lane with Long Hill, all dating back to the 1700s.

Southwards along Hall Moor Road, after crossing the disused standard gauge rail track bed leading to the Hall Dale Quarry the dwelling on the right was the laundry for Sir Joseph's Stancliffe Hall, and the reservoir in front of it supplied water to Stancliffe works at Whitworth Road.

The water which supplied the laundry and reservoir previously supplied the old Darley Hall in the adjacent field. The name for this, the second Darley Hall, was Nether Hall or Whitwell Hall. This spring on the east side of Hall Moor also supplied water to an underground reservoir in the field across the road. The reservoir fed the new Darley Hall fish pond and the Whitworth Park lakes.

At the bottom of the hill called Painters Nook, on the left, stands

DARLEY, DERBYSHIRE.

Particulars

OF AN EXCEEDINGLY VALUABLE

FREEHOLD ESTATE,

SITUATE IN THE PARISH OF DARLEY, IN THE COUNTY OF DERBY,

COMPRISING AN

EXCELLENT MANSION-HOUSE,

CALLED

"STONECLIFF HALL,"

With Gardens, Orchards, and Shrubberies, large Coach-houses and Stables, and every requisite convenience, delightfully situate in the romantic Vale of Darley Dale, and commanding a fine view, over its handsome pastures down a picturesque Valley, of the Parish Church, and a bold mountainous range of scenery, studded with Plantations of ornamental and lofty Timber Trees; one of the

FINEST QUARRIES IN THE KINGDOM,

OF

BEAUTIFUL WHITE FREE-STONE,

Possessing a durability equal to Granite, and of great extent.

THREE—EXCELLENT—FARMS,

A newly-erected and well-frequented

INN, called "THE GROUSE,"

AND SEVERAL VALUABLE PLOTS OF LAND WELL ADAPTED FOR THE SITE OF VILLAS.

The Estate extends to nearly 340 acres, which includes Pasture, Meadow, and Arable Land of superior quality, and extensive well-wooded Plantations; is distant 6 miles from Matlock, Bakewell, and Chatsworth respectively, and 9 from Chesterfield, (adjoining the high road leading from London to Manchester, by Matlock and Buxton,) and within a few minutes walk of the Manchester, Matlock, and Midland Junction Railway Station,

AND WILL BE SOLD BY AUCTION BY

MESSRS. SMITH & PEATY,

AT THE OLD BATH HOTEL,

At Matlock, Bath, in the said County of Derby,

On TUESDAY, the 24th day of JULY, 1855, at Five o'Clock in the Evening,

(SUBJECT TO SUCH CONDITIONS OF SALE AS WILL BE THEN AND THERE PRODUCED,)

IN ONE LOT.

DARLEY, DERBYSHIRE.

PARTICULARS

OF AN EXCEEDINGLY VALUABLE

FREEHOLD ESTATE,

Situate in the parish of Darley, in the county of Derby,

COMPRISING

AN EXCELLENT MANSION HOUSE, CALLED

STONECLIFF HALL,

With Gardens, Orchards, and Shrubberies,

Fit for the residence of a Gentleman of Fortune, having Large Coach Houses and Stables and every requisite convenience, delightfully situated in the romantic Vale of DARLEY DALE and commanding a fine view over its handsome Pastures down a Picturesque Valley of the Perrot Church and a bold mountainous range of scenery, studded with Plantations of Ornamental and Lofty Timber Trees;

ONE OF

The Finest Quarries in the Kingdom,

Of beautiful White Free-stone, possessing a durability equal to Granite, and of great extent;

THREE EXCELLENT FARMS,

And a newly-erected and well-frequented

INN, CALLED THE GROUSE.

THE WHOLE ESTATE EXTENDS TO NEARLY

400 ACRES;

WHICH INCLUDES

Pasture, Meadow, and Arable Land

OF SUPERIOR QUALITY,

And extensive well-wooded Plantations,

And is distant 5 miles from Matlock, Bakewell, and Chatsworth respectively, 9 from Chesterfield, and adjoins the High Road from London to Manchester, by Matlock and Buxton; which will be

SOLD BY AUCTION,

BY MR. BREAREY,

AT THE GROUSE INN, IN DARLEY AFORESAID,

On TUESDAY, the 5th day of OCTOBER, 1847,

AT FIVE O'CLOCK IN THE EVENING,

Wheatley House, home of the proprietor of James Smith & Sons, Nurserymen, for many years.

Turning right down Park Lane for two hundred metres there is the new entrance to the third and present Darley Hall on the right. This new Hall was built by Arkwright in 1790 and Judge Newall lived there before the Second World War. In the two World Wars the Hall was commandeered by the Ministry of Defence and occupied by the Army. In 1946/47 it was purchased by the Derbyshire County Council for use as a Maternity Hospital. Relinquished by the National Health Authority in 1990, it is now a private Residential Home.

Turning left at the junction of Park Lane with the B5057 leads you into the hamlet of Two Dales, known for many years as Toad Hole. The Old National School, now Hayes Bakehouse, is on the right. One hundred metres from the old school along the B5057 is a row of three dwellings, formerly one building known as the Reading Room. This was Two Dales's recreational building.

Adjacent to the Reading Room is the old Methodist Chapel, built in 1827, and opposite this is a house built in the mid 1700s by a member of the then prominent Dakeyne family which was used as a shop by the Derwent Valley Co-operative Society until 1968. Crossing over the Hall Dale brook on Peter's Bridge (named after one of Dakeyne's sons) and turning left immediately, facing you is the Plough Inn, another former Dakeyne house built for another son, Robert, and dated 1751. To the left of the Plough Inn at the bottom of Wheatley Road stood the Nags Head Inn, demolished in 1962. The very musical Holmes family lived here for many years. Before Peter's Bridge was constructed there was a ford.

On the B5057 on the same side as the Methodist Chapel was the Blacksmiths Inn dating back to 1633. Two hundred metres further along the B5057 is the junction on the right with Ladygrove Road where stands another Dakeyne house, the lintel over its door inscribed "Edward Dakeyne 1796".

Five hundred metres along Ladygrove Road towards Ladygrove Dale, on the right up a long drive stands Holt House, built in 1770/80, the principal home of the Dakeynes. Holt House was also a bank, known

as the Bank of   e, which issued its own bank notes, some of
which are still in use, ice today. The strong rooms in the semi-
basement area were intact until the 1970s. Holt House is a good
example of an unspoiled first class Georgian country house. Adjacent to
the house on the east is a large barn constructed in the style of a chapel,
with a stone dated 1416 above the door. The Dakeyne family motto was
"Strike Dakeyne, the devil's in the hemp", believed to originate from
naval fire ships – the Dakeynes had a history of naval service.

Continuing along Ladygrove Road and passing Denacre Lane on the
left is Dakeyne's Flax Mill of 1789 alongside the Ladygrove Brook.
The Flax Mill was driven by water power by a machine invented by the
Dakeynes (a disc engine), worked by a ninety-six feet head of water
which produced around thirty-five horse power. A patent for the
machine was granted in 1830. The mill, which is now fairly obscured by
modern buildings, is also a fine example of a textile mill of this era.
After passing the mill, on the right is a dwelling with a barn-like
building attached to it.This was the Darley Dale Mineral Water
Company, whose inscribed pop bottles, with glass marble stoppers, are
sometimes found in the area. Proceeding up the hill a modern
bungalow on the right marks the place where fourteen mill houses,
Loscoe Row, stood until the 1960s when they were demolished. At the
top of this very steep lane to the right is the original home of the
Dakeynes, Knab Hall.

John Dakeyne of Bonsall, son of Daniel also of Bonsall, settled in
Knabb Hall in 1716. John Dakeyne, who died in February 1777 aged 80,
founded a dynasty in Darley. Daniel, John's eldest son, acquired the
newly erected cotton mill at Ladygrove in 1789, together with its new
mill houses. The mill was equipped with 612 spindles and had space for
another 588. Daniel and his wife Isabel had nine children, including
Edward and James. Edward and James invented the Equalinum in 1794
and it was patented by their father Daniel, son of Daniel. As stated
previously, the Dakeynes ran their own Bank from Holt House. Their
mill business went bankrupt in June 1802. James had regained the mill
by 1839. By 1881 the flax mill business was over.

Miss Fogg at Springfield

Fogg's Hill. Victorian post box

Fircliffe 1900, home of the Dawson family, agent to Sir Joseph and Lady Whitworth

Wheatley House, Hallmoor Road, Two Dales. Smith Nursery family

Oddford Lane 1906

Reading Room, Two Dales. Now three dwellings with additions at each end 2001

Mr Bentley with horse and trap taxi 1900s

The old school, Two Dales 2001

Lanes taxi 1930

House on left, Hilda Burnett's chip shop

1950 B5057 Co-op delivery lorry. The wooden building was Mick Morris's furniture warehouse

The Holmes family at the Nags Head (a very musical family

The Nags Head. Now demolished

Mrs Norman with horse and trap outside the Nags Head

Mrs Pilkington in Wheatley Road above the Nags Head 1909

The Blacksmiths, Two Dales

Two Dales. Blacksmith with shop

Two Dales. Brook Bottom open

Two Dales. Brook Bottom in flood with butcher's shop on left

Two Dales. Brook Bottom closed

Old smithy at the Blacksmiths Arms, now a dwelling

Another Dekayne House opposite the Blacksmith's Inn

Knab House. The first Dakeyne house

The Holt which formed the Dakeyne's Bank of Darley Dale

The Plough, formerly Robert Dakeyne's house of 1751

Edward Dakeyne's house 1796

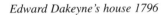

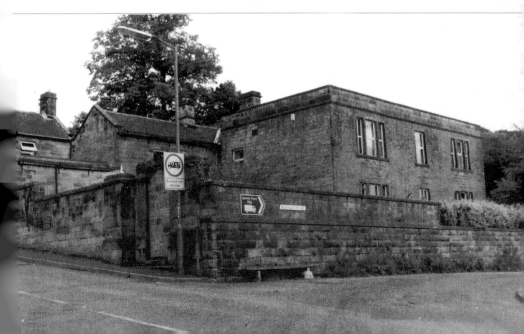

Johnson's Ladygrove Mill 2001

The fourteen houses of Loscoe Row and Knab House. Knab Quarry is in the background. It was also a parish quarry

Sydnope Hall 2001

Lady Grove Dale

Flash Dam 1970

Sydnope Hall was the residence of Sir Francis Darwin in 1826. He greatly improved the property. He laid out the grounds, constructing grottos, fountains, and created a lake (which came to be known as Flash Dam) covering 16 acres, with a boat house and pleasure boat.

The Sydnope Estate was approximately 200 acres. Sydnope Hall (2001) has been split into several private residences. The lake has been partially drained as a holiday village.

Flash Dam 2001

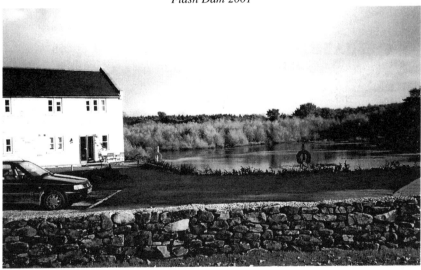

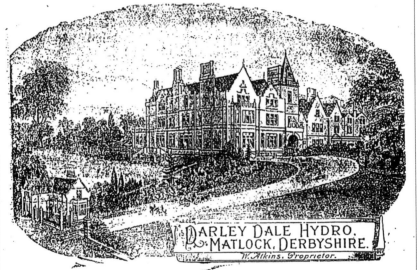

spacious and well-arranged stocked stables and coach houses. Mr. Atkins was for twelve years proprietor of the Rock Side Hydro., and he has an extensive experience in the practice of hydropathy according to the most approved methods. The baths at Darley Dale have been fitted up in the most complete manner, and facilities are at hand for vapour, Russian,sitz, needle, plunge and other baths, as well as for treatment by massage, &c. Patients have the advantage of being able to consult the physician of the establishment, Dr. W. Moxon, L.R.C.P., M.R.C.S., an eminent authority: and all the officials in the building, from the bathmen and bathwomen to the ordinary attendants, may be considered as more or less experts.

The surroundings are all of the most cheerful character: and with the refined home comforts and the admirable arrangements to save guests from the least trouble or inconvenience in making their arrangements or looking after the business details of their daily life, Darley Dale Hydropathic Establishment forms an ideal retreat for the weak, the tired or the ailing, as well as for the robust who are merely in search of a delightful holiday amid the most charming surroundings. In the comparatively short space of three years it has advanced into a leading position, and, mainly through Mr. Atkins' enterprise and ability, has become one of the most notable resorts in Derbyshire.

FAMOUS DERBYSHIRE HEALTH RESORTS
1893

A rather sad advertisement in the 'Buxton Advertiser'.

"The Hydro"

September 1904

The Creditors of the above-named WILLIAM ATKINS, who have not already sent in their CLAIMS, are required, on or before the 14th day of October, 1904, to send in their names and addresses and the particulars of their debts or Claims to Peter Gregson, of 37 Princess Street, in the City of Manchester.

Dated this 15th day of September, 1904.

ROBERT DAVIES and CO.,
Market Place, Warrington.
Solicitors for the above-named Trustee.

St Elphin's originally a hydro 1890

Normanhurst built in 1888 by Arthur Stanley Marsden Smedley who lived there until 1943. Acquired by Lehane, Mackenzie and Shand in 1953 for their head office until the late 1980s. It has now been converted into flats. The eleven acres of grounds are now a housing development

The mill was then let to a Mr Hope for the manufacture of twine. During the First World War the mill was used for training by the Leeds Rifles. The Dakeyne dynasty came to an end through the female heir and the estate was sold on 18th June 1924. Holt House has passed through several hands since.

At the top of Sydnope Hill on the B5057 on the right going towards Chesterfield stands Sydnope Hall accessed by a long drive flanked by an avenue of trees, originally a substantial Tudor farm house owned by the Dakeynes. This was sold to Sir Francis Darwin, uncle of Charles Darwin the author of "The origin of species", in the 1820s. Sir Francis radically extended the property. Sydnope Hall eventually came under the ownership of Sheffield City Council and was used as a home. This was later sold and was converted into a series of private dwellings in the 1980s.

The A6 between the Whitworth Institute building of 1890 and Darley's boundary with Matlock has some fine buildings alongside it. Between Greenaway Lane and Grove Lane is St. Elphin's School, formerly a large family house later demolished. In the 1880s a large Victorian house was built, known as The Grove, which was later considerably extended and became the Darley Dale Hydropathic Establishment.

On the opposite (west) side of the road is Normanhurst, built in 1888 by Arthur Stanley Marsden Smedley, who resided there until 1943. It was purchased in 1953 by the Civil Engineering firm Lehane, Mackenzie & Shand who sold it and its extensive grounds for development into private dwellings in the 1990s.

Just before the junction of the A6 with Hackney Lane, Darley House occupies an elevated position facing south on the east side of the A6. Two hundred metres below the junction with Hackney Lane, on the A6, is the Whitworth Hospital.

Looking across the valley to the south west from the Whitworth Hospital is the hamlet of Snitterton. The Domesday Book spelling is Sinitretone, thought to mean Snipe Town, referring to the birds which used to live on its marshy ground. Snitterton Hall is visible south of

Oker Hill. Two hundred and fifty metres to the east of the Hall is Snitterton Manor House, now a farm house. Entering the hamlet from Matlock on the Snitterton Road, just before an acute bend to the left there is a stone sign/mile post on the west side of the road. Thirty metres towards Oker there is a chapel-like building, and also a bull ring in the road. A small track on the west leads to Snitterton Hall

The Shirleys, who were located for generations at Snitterton after the Conquest, adopted the name Snitterton but also kept the name Shirley. The male issue of the Snitterton/Shirleys failed around the 1450s. The heiress married John Sacheverell of Ible. At the Reformation the Sacheverells purchased Darley Abbey for £26, which included fittings.

At the time of the dissolution of the monasteries there was a chapel in Snitterton attached to or near the original Manor House. At the rear of the old Manor House is some ancient part of a previous building. Snitterton Manor changed hands many times. One part of the Snitterton estate, including the old Manor House and the Hall were sold to Colonel John Millward. The other part was purchased by the Shores. When the Colonel died in 1670 his estate was split into three parts to provide for his three daughters. The oldest, Felicia, who retained the Hall and the Manor House, and her husband Charles Adderley sold their share, and there have been many subsequent owners.

Snitterton Road becomes Oker Road passing to the west of Oker Hill, eventually joining the B5057 opposite St. Mary's Church. Following the B5057 westwards up the hill for two hundred metres a track on the south leads to the Green, the site of the Wendesley family's home. Their Hall was demolished long ago. At the time of William the Conqueror Snitterton and Wensley were attached to Matlock, and are still part of the Soke and Wapentake of Wirksworth, ie the Wirksworth Hundred. The rest of the Darley Valley is in the High Peak Hundred, with the exception of Cowley. In the Domesday Book Wensley is spelled Wodnesleie. It is reputed to be "A clearing dedicated to Woden".

The Wendesleys were a knightly family of great military prestige, two of whose members sat in Parliament as Knights of the Shire, Thomas for four sessions in the 1300s and Richard twice in the 1500s.

Snitterton Hall 1603

Manor House Snitterton

Bull ring and stone mile/guide post

Oker Hill 1900s and the same view today 2001

Gated road, Darley Bridge to Oker, through Wenslees

Wooden house, Darley Bridge, formerly stood up the drive to Wenslees Farm

Wooden house now stone clad 2001

South Darley Village Hall

Cowley Hall first mentioned in the Domesday Book

HJ Enthoven & Sons works

Stanton Stand built to commemorate the 1832 Reform Act

One of the Wendesleys went to Jerusalem in the Crusades. About 1403, Sir Thomas de Wendesley, four times Knight of the Shire, took part, together with the vicar of Hope and others, in a dispute with Godfrey Roland, who lived at Longstone Hall. They went to his homestead and stole articles to the value of two hundred marks (£136.66). After taking Roland prisoner they carried him off to the Peak Castle at Castleton, which was used at that time (1403) for the detention of outlaws and criminals, where they kept him for six days without food and cut off his right hand. Sir Thomas de Wendesley was killed shortly afterwards at Shrewsbury fighting for Henry IV in the battle with the Earl of Northumberland, whose son Hotspur was also slain. The Wendesleys resided at Wensley for four hundred years, around sixteen or more generations. Richard de Wendesley, who was the last of the line, married Lettice Needham, whose family owned the nearby Cowley Hall from 1509 to 1613. Richard's death without issue left Lettice with the estate. She sold one part in 1591 to the Harpurs, and in 1613 sold the rest in four parts, one to Richard Senior, one to Roger Columbell and two to John Manners. The 1600s saw the end of the Darley valley's traditional lords and a fragmentation of their estates.

The old Manor of Cowley is one thousand metres from Darley Bridge, astride the road to the hamlet of Stanton Lees. It is in the Domesday Book as a manor in its own right. The entry reads "In Cowley Swein had 2 Bovates and Ultred 2 Bovates of Land taxable. Land for 4 oxen. 2 villagers and 1 smallholder have a plough. Meadow 4 acres. Underwood 1/2 league long and 2 furlongs wide. Value before 1066 and now 10s. Swein holds it. Ultred also held land at Elton". The now disused road to Birchover called Clough Lane passes to the west of Cowley Hall. The road from Darley Bridge to the junction with the Stanton Lees road is called Oldfield Lane. Cowley Hall in 1086 was retained by the King who let it to Henry de Ferrars together with Birchover, Elton and Gratton. In 1269 Henry III gave it to Gilbert de Collegh. It then passed to the Cadman family. In the reign of Henry VIII, Otwell Needham acquired Cowley by marrying the heiress. In 1613 it was sold to Richard Senior, who resided there. The heiress of Richard Senior married a Fanshaw and the Fanshaws held it until 1718 when it was sold to Thomas Bagshaw of Bakewell Hall. Three years later, in 1721, it became the property of William Fitzherbert of Tissington. The Fitzherberts held Cowley for twenty-eight years before selling it to George Wall, yeoman, of Darley in 1749. The Wall family in Darley had attended to their sheep shearing and tilling for six centuries, whilst the ambitious aspirations and improvidence of their neighbours had brought them only ruin. They had lived on in quietude and perpetuated their race. The Wall family still lives in Darley Dale. Sir Richard Arkwright purchased the Cowley Hall in 1791 and also purchased Snitterton and Darley Halls. Cowley Hall is now the administration building for H.J. Enthoven & Sons lead smelting works.

On the edge of Stanton Moor, on the western crest of the valley above and to the west of the hamlet of Stanton Lees, stands the Reform Tower, known locally as Stanton Stand. It was built to commemorate the 1832 Reform Act which gave the vote to men who were freeholders of property worth forty shillings a year, or those with land worth ten pounds annually, or who were leasing fifty pounds worth of property.

CHAPTER 3

COMMUNICATIONS, WATER AND POWER

ROADS

The roads at the turn of the twentieth century were an absolute mess of limestone dust and horse droppings, with a smelly choking dust cloud in dry times, and an even more smelly, sticky, muddy mess when it rained. All this ceased when the A6 was tarmacked in the 1920s.

The Darley district has numerous remnants of old roads and trackways. The A6 road bridge over the River Derwent at Rowsley on the down-stream side has built into the parapet wall a tablet marking the Rowsley/Darley boundary. Before the advent of the railway in 1848/9 the road which preceded the present A6 on leaving the Rowsley/Darley river bridge ran slightly to the south of the present A6 through what is now an industrial estate. It carried on over the present day A6 and went through the fields to link up with Cotehillock Lane near the junction with Tinkersley Lane.

The old road then carried on downhill until it met the present Northwood Lane. There is an old sign/mile post on the west side of this junction adjacent to the brook. The old road divided here into a high and a low route to Darley Church. The high route, portions of which are still in existence, followed a route from the old stone to the signpost about 100 metres to the east of the present A6 along the bottom of Sir Joseph Whitworth's North Park, passing through the Stancliffe Quarry area to join up with the present Church Lane leading to the church.

The low route turned westward at the stone signpost down todays Northwood Lane, across the A6, and what is now the Peak Rail railway track, adjacent to the river, then straight across the fields to the Church. This portion of the old road was called Derwent Lane and the rail crossing was named Nannygoat Crossing. Immediately over the rail crossing the pavers which used to form the road bed have been utilised to form part of a boundary wall. After passing through the fields the road comes to the property known as Abbey House, the original site of the Norman Darley family residence. There is another stone mile/sign post just over the wall in the private grounds of Abbey House. The road was officially abandoned in the early 1900s and is now only a public footpath until it reaches Churchtown School, and converges with Church Lane at the St. Helens Church. The old road now called Churchtown Lane carried forward until it met the present B5657 road, forming a crossroads. .

The road left to the north east (B5057) ascends until it meets and crosses the present day A6. This old road then went straight through what is now a housing estate, passing by both the present Darley Hall (Residential Home) and the site of the old Darley Hall (1321-1796), across the present Hall Moor Road, and made its way along the north side of the Hall Dale Valley (Hall Dale Lane), towards Chesterfield. In the 1700s this part of the lane was called Jaggers Lane and was a Gypsies' camp site in the nineteenth century. Now called Hall Dale Lane, it is a private road with a public footpath along it.

Returning to the A6 junction with the B5057, the B5057 was the route of another old road to Chesterfield running through the hamlet of Two Dales. After commencing the ascent of Sydnope Hill the road turns sharply to the left. The old road ran up what is now a drive on the left of the bend. This is private property with no right of way. A portion of the old road is known as Coxhead Lane and after a few hundred yards returned to the B5057 briefly before leaving it again opposite Denacre Lane to become a green road called Back Lane which leads to Darley Flash, past Woodside Farm. Two hundred metres from the green road junction with Sydnope Hill there is a large sign/mile post on the right,

Cote Hillock Lane 1921

Northwood, Cote Hillock junction 1921, used to be the main road from Rowsley to Matlock pre 1831

Cote Hillock junction 2001

Northwood, Cote Hillock junction 2001

Northwood Lane/Cotehillock signpost. Left of junction of Cotehillock Lane with Northwood Lane

Road at rear of Park Stores (2001) part of pre 1831 Matlock to Rowsley main road. This road ran from the top of Church Lane, through what is now part of Stancliffe Quarry, past the bottom of North Park at the rear of Park Stores, passing through Strutts Engineering works to link up with Cotehillock Lane

Church Lane/Green Lane junction 1930s

Green Lane 1930s

Back Lane signpost off Sydnope Hill

now used as a gatepost. Darley Flash was the site of a cattle and sheep market which was held on 13th May and 27th October.

Moor Farm was formerly an inn, where the market was held. Many of the old roads over the eastern Darley moors were drovers' roads, hence the wide grass verges which served both to drive the livestock on and to provide grazing .

Returning to the crossroads at the junction of Churchtown Lane and the B5057 the road leading to the A6 opposite to Churchtown Lane is called Old Road. It crossed the present A6 and went up what is now Greenaway Lane, leading to Hackney Road and serving the hamlet of Hackney, and then turned left up Amycroft Lane to the hamlet of Farley, then carrying forward and upwards, crossing the B5057 to meet the old green lane near Moor Farm, the site of the old market. This road is called Flash Lane.

Returning once more to the Churchtown/B5057 crossroads, turning right towards the Derwent, the road crosses Darley Bridge. Note that the arches have different shapes on the up and down sides of the river. This is where the former ford was, as the river is wide and shallow at this point. About one mile upstream, just south of the Firth Rixson steel factory there is another fordable place across the river. This was served by a road, now strictly private, leading from just west of the convergence of the River Wye with the Derwent. This road went across the river and joined Derwent Lane, and also continued forward to serve Stanton Woodhouse high on the west slopes of the valley. Where the road leaves the river bridge at Darley Bridge going west once again there was a high and a low route, leading to Matlock and the south. The low route runs parallel with the Derwent along a single track gated road, called Wenslees at the bridge end and Aston Lane at the Snitterton end, to the hamlets of Oaker and Snitterton, where it joins the high route which followed the B5057 from Darley Bridge half a mile up the west side of the valley to Cross Green where the high route turns left, to pass west of Oaker Hill and joins the low route to Snitterton and Matlock.

Passing through the hamlet of Snitterton, with its two ancient manor houses, the road bends sharply left. Just past the private road to

Snitterton Hall there is another guide/mile-post on the right. There is also a bull ring in the road near this point.

Another old and now forgotten road, abandoned in the 1870s, is one which ran from a point where Church Lane met the A6 to Northwood. The road passed through the property called West Lodge, across Sir Joseph's Lane, past Fircliffe and continued up through Stancliffe Hall grounds, to Stancliffe Hall, then on to Northwood. A portion of this now strictly private lane can be seen at the end of Fircliffe Lane off Whitworth Road and at the top of Whitworth Road. This road went out of use in the 1870s when Sir Joseph Whitworth had it replaced with a new road known as Whitworth Road, to give himself more privacy at the Hall. Re-routing the road caused the people from the hamlet of Northwood to walk an extra half mile to attend Church.

Two hundred metres before Whitworth Road meets the junction with Bent Lane and Northwood Lane, the western side wall changes character from typical Derbyshire stone walling to the Whitworth coursed stone, with its half round masoned coping. The point at which

Darley Bridge 1929. Steam lorry rans-porting spar from Mill close Mine

it changes is where the old road went down through the fields to the Hall and Church Lane. This coursed walling was standardised by Whitworth for use on his estate and can be seen all over Darley.

Returning to and passing over Darley Bridge on the B5057 about 120 metres west from the bridge you come to Oldfield Lane on the right. This leads to the hamlets of Cowley and Stanton Lees and Birchover. The first turn off to the left on this lane (approx. 400 metres from the B5057) is the old road to Birchover, still a public road but now fallen into disuse

Moor Farm, Flash Lane. The site of a cattle and sheep fair in the 1700-1800s. 13th May and 27th October

Darley Bridge from the air 1981

Watt's engine boiler flues

Old Millclose Mine 2001. Watt's engine house with Watt's shaft to the left

Old lead miners' footpath from Sabine Hey to Warren Car

Old road to Birchover and Sabine Hey

Oldfield Lane, behind Enthovens, part of the old road to Birchover

Hill Carr Sough

103

since the demise of Millclose Mine. This road is certainly not to be recommended for vehicles. The A6 was realigned and renovated between 1828 and 1831. A new bridge was built over the Hall Dale/Ladygrove brook near Warney Lea. The adjacent corn mill leat also had a new bridge. The site of the old Warney Cornmill is now the home of the DFS Furnishing Company.

A toll house, now demolished, was erected at the same time on the A6 at its junction with Old Road, just south of the Greenaway Lane junction. A new coaching inn was built on the A6 near the Whitworth Road junction, the Grouse Inn. The next toll house northwards was in Great Rowsley parish. It is still in existence, the last single storey building on the right as one leaves the village towards Bakewell.

CANALS

The Industrial Revolution included a transport revolution, which began with the building of Britain's canals, mostly constructed between 1770 and 1810. This forty-year period of canal building did for Britain what the motorway building programne has done in the forty years since the early 1960s. Derbyshire, despite its hilly terrain, has a number of well known canals. One of the shortest was the one mile long Woodeaves Canal of 1802, north of Ashbourne, running parallel to the Bradbourne Brook. The Chesterfield Canal, built between 1771 and 1777 is some forty-five and a half miles long, with sixty-five locks and two tunnels. The Erewash Canal, 1777-1791, is two and a half miles long with fourteen locks. The Trent and Mersey Canal, 1766-1777, had very busy inland port at Shardlow. The Derby Canal was constructed 1791-1796. The Peak Forest Canal, 1794-1798, was some fourteen miles long, and a rail connection ran between this canal and the Cromford Canal, called the High Peak Railway.

Our nearest canal is the Cromford Canal of 1794, which has one tunnel and two aqueducts It was built to carry limestone from the Crich quarries to Jessop & Outram's iron foundry at Butterley. The canal extended to serve Arkwright's Cromford mills. It became an extremely busy, profitable canal. Thousands of tons of stone from Hopton and Stancliffe Stone Quarry, were shipped all over the country from Cromford wharf, including the great lions, sculpted in Darley Dale, which crouch at the entrance to St. George's Hall, Liverpool. St. George's Hall is featured in the television series Brookside's opening title shots. The lions were delivered from Darley Dale to Cromford by cart, then by canal to Liverpool. Hundreds of tons of lead also made the short journey by boat to the smelter at Lea, via the Lea extension to the Cromford Canal. This extension also served Smedley' s Mills.

The Darley valley also has one of the first Derbyshire canals, 1776 to 1787. This canal was based on the Worsley section of the Bridgewater Canal (1759-1761), which commenced in and drained Worsley coal mines and transported the coal to Manchester. The canal/sough was conceived by John Gilbert, the Duke of Bridgewater's agent at Worsley, and engineered by James Brindley, a Derbyshire man from Tunstall near Wormhill, who is said to be the father of canal construction in Britain.

Only five years after the completion of the Worsley-Manchester section of the Bridgewater canal in 1761 a group of men with interests in lead mining and smelting in Derbyshire decided to construct a drainage system to de-water the Youlgreave lead-mining area. Prominent among these men were Peter Nightingale of Lea and John Barker of Bakewell, lead smelters and mine owners. They recruited Gilbert and Brindley. John Barker visited the Worsley coal mines on behalf of the shareholders, who included the Dukes of Rutland and Devonshire.

It was decided to drive a canal some two and one third miles long under Stanton Moor towards Youlgrave from the west bank of the Derwent opposite the point now occupied by the Firth Rixson steelworks. The canal was primarily for drainage but was to be capable of navigation by long boats, and boats were responsible for transporting approximately thirty thousand tons of waste from the canal working. The last time working miners used the canal was in 1938/9, when they were investigating the origin of the water flooding Millcose Mine at that time, and this drainage channel, or sough, known as the Hillcar Sough, has become Derbyshire's forgotten canal

Work on the sough/canal was commenced in 1776. An adjustable weir was constructed to govern the water level at the junction with the River Derwent together with mooring bays for the long boats used to transport the debris from the tunnel, and unloading facilities and roads for the disposal of the debris. The size of the long-boats were to be no larger than 3' wide and 36' long. These long-boats were known as "starvation boats" because all their ribs were visible The same type of boat was used on the Bridgewater canal at the Worsley coal mines.

The strata the sough/canal passed through was mostly composed of shale. This was comparatively easy to excavate but contained methane gas and was very wet. The decision was made to line the tunnel with masonry from nearby Stancliffe Quarry. The minimum dimensions of the tunnel were 6'1" wide and 7'7" high, with proposed sections 10' wide for passing etc. A natural stony shelf in the Derwent enabled the river to be easily forded near the sough entrance. A way from Derwent Lane in Darley Dale was purchased for transportation of the stone. Owing to the availability of stone from Stancliffe Quarry to line it, the proposed route of the sough was abandoned in favour of a circular route that ran alongside, not through, the limestone mass that is under the Stanton Moor gritstone cap.

By 1769 the tunnel had progressed one thousand yards (914 metres). Because of its great depth below Stanton Moor it was not practicable to sink an air shaft so ventilation proved very difficult. In 1774 a methane gas explosion injured several men. In 1775 the sough encountered several large springs which lowered the water table at Stoney Lee Mine. In 1777 six men died through gas problems, and in 1778/9 the Stanton Moor air shaft was sunk $1^3/4$ miles from the entrance to relieve ventilation difficulties.

The boatmen were paid ls.2d (6p) per day and miners received one shilling (5p) per day. The men who kept the bottom of the sough/canal free from mud and debris were paid two shillings (10p) per day. These men worked all day wet through and very cold. Conditions were absolutely appalling and to keep the men the owners gave them gifts of ale, rum and food, also free candles. Usually the men had to either buy or make their own candles. It must have been terrifying to work in the tunnel before the ventilation shaft was sunk.

Tradition has it that the boatmen carried yew and holly branches up the sough with them, and on the return journey down the sough spread them out to make a fan-like plug around the boat to increase the ventilation by pushing out the bad air. Fresh air was supplied to the far end of the tunnel by wooden trunking.

By 1783 the tunnel had reached Greenfield Farm near the Alport to Elton road, a distance of 4,218 yards (2 miles) of good navigable canal. Another air shaft was sunk there to further improve ventilation. In 1787, twenty-one years after commencement, the sough reached Guy Shaft and the Hillcarr Sough was considered finished as the main drain for the Youlgreave/Alport area. In April of that year a party was held to celebrate the completion of the sough. Copious amounts of ale and rum were provided, two sheep and an ox were roasted, and between four and five hundred people attended. Needless to say after completing one of the wettest, most hazardous jobs one could ever imagine, it rained all day at the party.

The venture had cost around £32,000, lowered the water table by sixty-five to seventy feet in the Alport area, and paid for itself in two years. Eventually the sough and its various branches totalled over four miles long and brought the overall cost up to around £50,000.

The last extension made to the Hillcarr Sough was to Mawstone Mine, Youlgreave, in 1882, ninety-five years after its completion. Once again ventilation, gas and water problems were encountered. Just how severe the water problems were is illustrated by the following, taken from an old book on Youlgreave.

In 1882 a man went into Mr. Guilder's house at Bakewell (which later became Howards Shop) and informed them that a huge hole had opened up by the big tor (Rainstor Rock at Alport) and a milk cart had gone down it. The hole became as large as a house, swallowing up the River Bradford. People came from far and wide to view the spectacle.

A man from Baslow with a black retriever foolishly threw a stick into the water. The strong current swept the dog down the hole, and three weeks later the remains of the dog were found in the Derwent at Darley Dale. The hole was finally made up by choking it with brush-wood followed by loads of stone.

In 1932 five miners and three would-be rescuers were killed by gas and explosion at Mawstone Mine, which was then closed, bringing to an end after one hundred and forty-five years the use of Hillcarr for draining working lead mines. The closing of the Millclose Mine in 1939 (ironically through water problems) effectively finished two thousand years of lead mining in Derbyshire.

Today approximately eight million gallons of water a day enter the Derwent from Hillcarr Sough, enhancing the Derwent's flow with a staggering twelve million tons of water per year.

The Minute Book of the Hillcarr Sough Company contains some very interesting items. In 1777 there is a list of twelve miners under the heading "Never more to be employed". This was the year of the tragedy when six miners were killed by gas. It is believed these twelve miners refused to work Sundays in order to keep the ventilation system working. The names of these and other lead miners who worked on the Sough are still common around here today.

Dennis Wild deceased, lead miner of Winster, had in his possession a glass goblet inscribed "Good luck to the Hillcarr Sough". Its whereabouts, and whether there are any other such goblets, are unknown to me.

Throughout the long history of lead mining, water and gas have been the main enemies. Mans ingenuity has been stretched to the limit to overcome these hazards.

The last known journey by lead miners up the Hillcarr Sough took place in 1938/9 to ascertain if the great influx of water which eventually closed Millclose Mine could be coming from a leak in the sough. The under-manager of Millclose, Mr. Trail, borrowed a rowing boat from the trustees of the Whitworth Institute, and accompanied by miners Dick Slack, Ben Brassington and Bill Stringer, they examined the sough. I was surprised to learn from Bill Stringer, when he related this episode to me in 1999, that the sough, according to his memory, passed through a very high and wide section. No leaks were found, and no gas encountered. One hundred and sixty years after its completion according to Bill the sough was still in reasonable order, a tribute to the skills of the men who constructed it.

Darley Water Works. Cast iron sign dating from 1904. Darley Water Works was at White Springs Farm, Bent Lane near Bumper Castle Farm.
These signs are still to be seen at Blind Lane, Hackney, Northwood Lane, Darley Dale, and at the Hall Dale brook footpath

It is recorded that the success of the sough/canal at Worsley coal mine also led to the scheme to construct an underground canal in Speedwell Mine at Castleton in Derbyshire for the purpose of transporting lead ore. A sum of around £14,000 was expended on the project, which proved to be a failure, with the promoters losing all their money. The Speedwell Mine is open to visitors, who travel the canal to view the so-called bottomless pit and the great cascade, and wonder at the skills and ingenuity of the Derbyshire lead miners of the late 1770s who carried out the work.

RAILWAYS

The railway came to Darley Dale from Ambergate in 1848 and terminated in Little Rowsley in the parish of Darley Dale. Joseph Paxton designed the terminus station, which is still standing today, as part of the new shopping village adjacent to Chatsworth Road, built on the site of the original 1849 railway terminus. 1869 saw the completion of the line to Manchester and the construction of a new station on the opposite side of the A6.

In the 1920s a loco shed, built to accommodate approximately twenty-seven locos, now demolished, was constructed adjacent to the west side of what is now Firth Rixson's steel factory. A marshalling yard, with extensive railway sidings, occupied the area between Derwent Lane's Nannygoat crossing and the new and Paxton's old station.

The railway entrance to the Paxton station and yard was by way of a short tunnel under the A6. The Manchester line crossed the A6 by means of a bridge, now demolished, close by the east side of the road/river bridge, then one hundred metres north crossed the Derwent by another bridge, still standing, before proceeding to Bakewell.

Going north over the river/road bridge, immediately turning left for Pillough there is another road bridge over the River Wye, making a total of six past and present bridges within a two hundred metres radius of the A6 river/road bridge. The A6 road, the river Derwent and railway also merge at the bottom of Northwood Lane and at the south boundary of Darley Dale where the railway crosses the Derwent by an iron bridge.

Darley Dale also had a small railway siding on the south side of Darley Station and the B5057, where goods were trans-shipped to and from destinations all over Britain. The nursery, timber, stone and coal trades kept this small sidings very busy for one hundred years, from 1850 to the 1950s.

Stancliffe Estates and Stone Quarries also had a private standard gauge railway approximately two miles long linked to the main line. Two locos, an 040 and an 060, served the Hall Dale and Stancliffe Quarry areas, passing under the A6 at the southern end of Peakland View, Darley

Engine sheds 1930s

Static converted coaches used for sports and recreation facilities

Dale, now a pedestrian sub-way, and ascending by a loop line across the Hallmoor Road to the Hall Dale Quarries approximately one hundred metres elevation above Darley Dale station main line.

John Gregory & Sons, timber merchants of Old Road, ran teams of shire horses and timber drugs. They also had two steam traction engines. Several local people ran horse-drawn charabancs and conveyances, catering for the large number of visitors who came by rail to Paxton's station at Little Rowsley between 1850 and 1869 to visit the Peak District and view its scenery and stately homes. Excursion trains also ran to the Darley Whitworth Park up to the First World War.

PEAK RAIL

The Railway through Darley valley opened for traffic as far as Rowsley on 4th June 1849. The name of the Company was Manchester, Buxton, Matlock and Midland Junction Railway. The name was almost as long as the line. Darley Dale station was originally built on the south side of Station Road around 1850. A new more impressive station was constructed in 1874 on the north side of Station Road at a cost of £2,247.85 and is still in good condition today. Loop lines and sidings were added to serve local industries. Passenger use increased from 13,000 in 1872 to 44,000 in 1902. The other two stations, both known as Rowsley, were actually in the then Parish of Darley Dale. The end of the line came in 1968 when the lines, sleepers and infrastructure were removed. The station was used for light industry for a period after 1968 including the manufacture of model locos. A group of rail enthusiasts got together with a view to the restoration of the line. Their first job was to make sure that local authorities, who had purchased the track, were made aware of the viability of restoring the track to its former use. In 1987 serious efforts began towards the eventual aim of reinstating the line and in 1988 Peak Rail plc .came into being. By 1997 a single track ran from Matlock to the site of the demolished engine sheds at Northwood, behind Firth Rixson's steel works. Construction work at this site is ongoing and has been named Rowsley South.

WATER, SANITATION AND POWER

On the eastern valley slopes the spring line is about one hundred metres below the gritstone moorland cap at an elevation around five hundred to six hundred feet (150-180 metres). These springs provided a supply of good clean water essential for people's needs. Numerous local water distribution points and schemes were in operation prior to 1904, when Darley Dale Council's piped water supply was established from the aptly named Whitespring Farm on the east side of the Hall Dale Brook, opposite Bumper Castle Farm.

Whitesprings, accessed from Bent Lane and Flash Lane, was farmed by Jonathan Barker until 1904 – farming ceased when the Council's water works was set up. A pipeline ran alongside the Hall Dale Brook, then under the path/trackway which became the present Hall Dale Lane. There are still a number of cast iron markers for the pipeline stop taps in existence in places as far apart as Hackney Road, Blind Lane, Northwood Lane and Hall Dale Lane, all bearing the legend D.D.W.B. The small building which housed the water filtration system at Whitesprings is still there. The Whitesprings farm house and outbuildings, which were still intact in the 1930s, have largely been demolished for their stone over the years since then. The Whitesprings level was approximately eight hundred feet (240 metres) elevation, so ensuring a good head of water to Darley in general.

In a later reorganisation the Severn Trent Water Board took over all local water sources and supplies and Whitesprings was phased out. Darley's drinking water is now mostly supplied from the Derwent Valley dams by the pipe-line which passes above Darley Hillside to feed the large underground reservoir at Crich. From Crich the water then goes on to supply Derby, Leicester and Nottingham.

The Derwent Valley Water Board four feet (1200 mm) dia-twin pipe-line was constructed around 1912. It enters Darley Dale after crossing the Beeley/Little Rowsley road two hundred metres south of Beeley. During the construction a railway track was laid from Rowsley old Goods Yard, passing through Chatsworth Park to the valve house at Baslow, which is situated two hundred metres north east of the

Guide hut at Lumb Lane, Northwood (1970) believed to be from Birchin Lee, formerly a workmens' hut for the tunnellers working on the 1912 Derwent Valley pipelines from Derwent Dams to Crich.
This tunnel passes some 220ft below Burley Fields Farm and comes out in the Hall Dale wood.
Original Guide hut now replaced

Darley Hillside, Showing Cobb Slater's Cosim works, Green Lane Triangle, and Vine Yard Terrace

Hallmoor Road 1977. Site of second Darley Hall 1321 called Nether Hall, Hall Farm, Wheatley House and Nursery. Site of James Smith packing shed, now Porteous Close. Foreground 1927 chapel and Blacksmith Inn

Vineyard Terrace, Hallmoor Road, 1912. The author was born at number three in 1927

Hall Moor Road, top of Gill Lane 1900s

Hall Moor Road. 50 metres west from the top of Gill Lane 1900s

1900s

100 years in the life of a house (1900-2000) at Hall Moor Road. Formerly the home of Norman Gregory, 50 metres from the top of Gill Lane, now called Barrowcote

1920s

1940s

1980

Sheffield/Chesterfield traffic island. A rail junction near Beeley served a rail cable incline which pulled the pipes up the hill on railway wagons to a point near the acute bend on the Rowsley Bar road, where another valve house is situated.

The water then passes through Copywood and Tinkersley to Northwood by means of a cut-and-fill 6'3" (1900mm) diameter blue brick culvert. At Northwood

House dated 1667 at Northwood hamlet

it enters a valve house at Lumb Lane just below the Guide Headquarters building. From the valve house the culvert turns into a proper tunnel of the same blue brick construction, passing under Darley Hillside two hundred feet (61 metres) deep below the farmland west of Burley Fields Farm. The tunnel/conduit emerges above the Hall Dale Lane approximately one hundred metres west of Hall Dale Quarry into a syphon inlet house. The length of this section of the tunnel/conduit is approximately one mile (1600 metres). On leaving the Hall Dale syphon house the water returns to twin four feet (1200 mm) steel pipes. The syphon pipe-line then passes under the Hall Dale Brook up Sydnope Hill to the B5057, on the bends one hundred and twenty feet up from the Ladygrove Road junction, carrying onward and passing under Ladygrove Road and Brook near the drive to Holt House to arrive at the syphon outlet house above the end of Holt Lane. The water then flows through another blue brick 6'3" tunnel/conduit one and a half miles in length which passes under Farley Farm, emerging approximately one hundred metres west of the A623 Chesterfield Road/Asker Lane junction. One mile of this Holt Lane to Matlock tunnel/conduit is in Darley Parish. At regular intervals pipeline inspectors walk miles of tunnel for inspection purposes.

Two camps were set up for the excavation and construction of these

119

tunnels. The Lumb Lane tunnel entrance camp had stables for the pit ponies, which were used to remove the spoil, and the tunnellers lived in a large corrugated iron building brought here from Birchin Lee, the Derwent Valley Dams temporary village. This building remained on the site and was given to the Scouting Association and used as a Guide Hut until the 1970s when it was replaced by a building on the same site. The other camp was at Farley, above the Holt Lane syphon house.

North Darley's first foul sewer system was installed by Sir Joseph Whitworth in the 1870s. Darley and Matlock Urban District Councils improved and extended the system over the years. The last improvement was carried out by Lehane, Mackenzie and Shand between 1962 and 1964. South Darley had environmental problems in the 1900s with a lack of an adequate sewerage system. Night-soil lorries remained in operation in north and south Darley until the early 1960s in outlying areas.

Town gas came to Darley from the Matlock Gas Works situated between the Hooleys Estate and the Dimple Road junction on the A6, which was established in 1853. The Gas Works has now closed and gas is now supplied from the national grid.

Mains electricity arrived in Darley Dale around 1930. Stancliffe Works had generated their own from 1923, overseen by a man called Billy Bell. They also had an electric accumulator battery charging station. The batteries were used to power doorbells, telephones and wirelesses.

CHAPTER 4

HEALTH AND HAPPINESS

RECREATION

Every village in the Middle Ages had a piece of land set aside by law to practice archery. The area usually came to be known as The Butts. This name is still extant in the road near Churchtown. Darley Dale has a thriving Archery Club which practices near Darley Bridge. Pigeon racing, poultry clubs, football, tennis, bowls and cricket have been established for over one hundred years in Darley & District together with billiards, snooker and dancing. Evening classes, encompassing all matter of educational activities were held in the Whitworth Institute, established by Sir Joseph Whitworth's legatees in 1890. Darley Band, Horticultural Society and a lending library were also based at the Whitworth Institute. The recreational building called the Reading Room (1849-1890) was situated at Two Dales next door to a former Methodist Chapel and later converted to three dwellings. The functions of the Reading Room were taken over by the new Whitworth Institute in 1890. Public houses abounded in Darley Dale and District, together with a few beer houses.

The Railway Companies also catered for their workers on the land where Firth Rixson now stands. It comprised of a sports field for football, cricket and tennis. Two old railway coaches, mounted on timber trestles, were used as changing rooms, for whist drives and as a tea pavilion.

South Darley had a Reading Room to the north west of Wensley Square. The building is still there. A new Reading Room near to the top of Wensley was built in 1891 by money provided by Joseph and Sarah Taylor. The inscription above the door translates as "Sweet is the place of one's birth". Very apt for anyone fortunate enough to be born and live here in our lovely valley. The Darley Dale Band originated in the old Reading Room at Wensley on 16th August 1880. It was then called Wensley Brass Band and changed its name to Darley Dale United Brass Band when it moved to the Whitworth Institute in 1898. Up to the Second World War Wensley, like Snitterton, had a bull ring. Wensley's was in the Square.

The name of Oker supposedly dates from the time when the hill was a Roman station called Occursus, or Hill of Conflict. Roman artefacts and coins have been found on Oker Hill and there is evidence of earth works on the hill. Although a splendid place to build a castle or large fortified building none has ever been constructed there because of the poor quality of the ground (shale).

SIR JOSEPH WHITWORTH

Joseph Whitworth, born 1803, was the epitome of the self-made Victorian industrialist. His mother died when he was eleven and his father Charles had Joseph and his brother John fostered. Their infant sister was sent to an orphanage in Bristol. Joseph's early years in the back streets of of Stockport, and having to fend for himself, endowed him with self-reliance and a radical outlook on life. Whitworth is believed to have started work at a cotton mill in the Ambergate area. He moved to Manchester around 1820/21, then to London in 1825, marrying Frances Ankers, the illiterate daughter of a canal barge-master from Tarvin in Cheshire, in Ilkeston, Derbyshire. Frances was to die as Lady Whitworth in obscurity, near Tarvin. Whitworth worked for, and alongside, some of the great mechanical engineers of the 19th century. He returned to Manchester in 1832/33 and set up in business as Joseph Whitworth Tool Maker. His persistence, ingenuity and drive for

Sir Joseph Whitworth

Lady Whitworth

perfection led to immense riches and status.

In 1853, on behalf of the British Government, he visited America to study their method of manufactury (making use of largely unskilled labour). The outcome was the "Special Report on the American Method of Manufactury, presented to the House of Commons by Mr. Joseph Whitworth by command of Her Majesty Queen Victoria, on 6th February 1854." Whitworth concluded the report with the following. "Wherever education and an unrestricted press are allowed full scope to exercise their united influence, progress and improvement are the certain results, and among the many benefits which arise from their joint co-operation may be ranked most prominently the value which they teach men to place upon intelligent contrivance; the readiness with which they cause new improvements to be received, and the impulse which they thus unavoidably give to that inventive spirit which is gradually emancipating man from the rude forms of labour, and making what were regarded as the luxuries of one age to be looked upon in the next as the ordinary and necessary conditions of human existence." He

To Wish you
a very Happy Christmas
and a Bright New Year.

Lady Whitworth,
Cannes.

1893.

Wishing you a very Merry Christmas and in the coming year health and happiness

Lady Whitworth
Hotel Beau Séjour Cannes

was invited to spend Christmas 1856 with Queen Victoria and Prince Albert at Osborne House. Stancliffe Hall, Darley Dale, was purchased by Joseph at this time and so began his involvement with Darley Dale. Joseph was knighted in 1869.

Sir Joseph and his wife Frances had lived apart for many years, and six months after her death in November 1870 he married his long-time friend Mary Louisa Orrell, a widow aged forty-one years. Sir Joseph and Lady Louisa made Stancliffe Hall their main residence. Joseph Dawson was Sir Joseph's agent and estate manager and on Sir Joseph's instruction purchased as much of Darley Dale as he could.

Sir Joseph was a philanthropist in life and death, making many gifts

STANCLIFFE.

These Christmas cards were from Lady Whitworth to Daisy Woolliscroft nee Watson, who was a maid at Stancliffe Hall 1890s

To Wish you
a very Happy Christmas
and a Bright New Year.

Mary L. Whitworth,
Cannes.

towards improving education in his lifetime. When he died in January 1887 aged 84 he left his fortune to his wife and two friends, to spend "in accordance with his wishes". Sir Joseph and Lady Whitworth, and his step-daughter Mary's graves are in St. Helen's Church-yard.

THE WHITWORTH LEGACY

The people of Darley and District benefitted from the legacy with the Whitworth Institute and the Whitworth Hospital. The Whitworth Institute, now called the Whitworth Centre, opened in October 1890. The present Whitworth Hotel, formerly called Whitworth House, was used by the North Darley Urban District Council, the Sheffield and Rotherham Bank, the Cottage Gardening and Industrial Society, and the Cricket Club. Lady Louisa died in St. Pancras Hotel, London, in May 1896 and a company called Stancliffe Estates purchased practically all the Whitworth Estate.

Whitworth had built a large model farm at the junction of Whitworth Road and the A6 (now an industrial estate) which was converted into a masons and stone sawing yard. At the rear of the farm stood a very large cowhouse which in 1898 was taken down and re-erected close to the football field in Whitworth Park. It was 112 feet long (34 metres) by 32 feet wide (10.42 metres), and a kitchen and toilets were added. The building was used as an exhibition centre and refreshment rooms for parties. It was demolished in the 1960s because of repeated vandalism. The reservoir which fed the boating lake was situated near the site of the second Darley Hall and held fifty thousand gallons. A steel main from the reservoir ran to the Whitworth through what is now a housing estate. In the Whitworth building there was a comprehensive lending library, a museum, a games room, and a swimming pool 55 feet (16.45 metres) by 25 feet (7.62 metres) and 6 feet 6 inches (2 metres) to 3 feet 6 inches (1.06 metres) deep. Educational activities included classes as diverse as shorthand and typing, carpentry, swimming, science and art, choral classes, dancing, dressmaking, geology, first aid, and gardening.

On 1st September 1894 the Whitworth Monument was unveiled. It

The Whitworth Institute

Stancliffe Hall House Staff 1880s

Back row, l to r: 1. Ben Bonsall, 2. Daisy Watson (Wooliscroft), 3. ? 4. ? 5. Mr. Gold, 6. ? 7. John Wood,
Front row, l to r: 1. Mrs Jack Sam Allsop, 2. ? 3. Mrs Murdoch (housekeeper), 4. ? 5. ?

Stancliffe Hall Garden Staff 1880s

Standing, l to r: 1. John Wilson (Bill, Roger and Jack Wilson's grandfather), 2. John Siddall, 3. Henry Condiffe (Bill Needham's grandfather), 4. George Smith (Edward Smith's father), 5. Bill Mason (Mrs Corfield's brother) Seated, l to r: 1. Jack Sam Allsop (Laurie Twigg's uncle), 2. Henry Fearn (Bertha Fearn's grandfather), 3. William Barker (Two Dales), 4. Walter Wall (John Wall's father), 5. Harry Fielding (Jack Fielding's father)

The Weeping Elm, Whitworth Institute Grounds.   Darley Dale.

The Whitworth Institute

Whitworth Institute and Monument, Darley Dale.

Whitworth Hospital

was also the day of the annual Cottage Gardens Society Show, and between seven and eight thousand people attended on the day. The Park was laid out by Mr. Joseph Dawson, Whitworth's agent, who trained under Sir Joseph Paxton. From 1890 to 1898 the Whitworth Institute was run by governors. On 6th October 1898 the Whitworth Institute and its endowments were handed over to fourteen trustees. On the same day the Whitworth Hospital and its endowments were handed over to another band of fifteen trustees. The Whitworth Hospital and its endowment became part of the National Health Service after the Second World War. Both facilities were for use by the people of Darley Dale and, at the discretion of the trustees, adjoining or neighbouring parishes. Mr. Brooke-Taylor proposed the vote of thanks to the legatees of Sir Joseph. Mr. Herbert Brooke-Taylor was a founder member of the Two Dales Reading Room, and Brooke-Taylors were trustees of the Whitworth Institute for around eighty years. Her Grace the Duchess of Rutland attended the ceremony. Mr. Darbishire in his speech mentioned that some of the young people of the area were "rather a rough lot. There was a violence of language, some intemperance, and other things perhaps more deplorable." It was thought that by giving them good

133

entertainment and a billiards/games room, without any what is called drink available, it would improve their manners, speech and behaviour.

In the First World War the Whitworth Institute was used as a hospital for wounded soldiers. After the 1914-18 war many classes and the Cottage Gardening Society were never revived. At the beginning of the Second World War the Whitworth Institute was once again requisitioned, this time by the Army. A number of soldiers evacuated from Dunkirk came in 1940. The Whitworth eventually became an R.A.S.C. driver training camp and many nissen huts and some brick buildings were erected in the park. Several soldiers who were at the Whitworth Institute in the First and Second wars married local girls and settled in the area. After the Second war the Whitworth was very run down. Shortage of money caused the boating lake and the swimming baths to close. Over the next fifty years the endowments have mostly been sold to subsidise the upkeep of the building and the park. It is intended that the trustees will hand over the Whitworth in its entirety to Darley Dale Town Council in 2002.

EXTRACTS FROM ST. HELEN'S, DARLEY, MAGAZINE, 1890
Darley Dale Cottage-Gardening and Industrial Society

A meeting was held in the Reading Room, Two Dales, on Friday evening, August 29th, for the purpose of receiving the Report of the recent Exhibition, and distributing the prizes awarded. The Rector, as Chairman of the Committee, presided.

The Secretary having read the report (which is printed below), the Chairman proceeded to make some remarks on the advantages which the parishioners ought to gain from the annual holding of such Exhibitions. He thought that the recent show had on the whole fully maintained the standard reached in the previous year. The largely increased number of entries for the prizes offered for garden-culture was a matter for congratulation. A well-managed cottage-garden represented a good many things, eg, a variety of healthful food, healthy exercise, useful occupation, a safe-guard against the temptations of idleness; and, where flowers were cultivated as well as vegetables, a great deal of pure pleasure and refining influence was to be had. The number of entries in the Industrial Section had been disappointing, except in the children's work, but the quality of the few exhibits there were seemed to shew an advance both in skill and in good taste. He had tried to ascertain the cause of the falling-off in the number of mechanical objects sent in for competition, and he had good reason to believe that the prizes offered were in some cases much too small to induce men to spend time and money in competing for them. He thought that if the objects aimed at, viz., encouragement of industry, and development of taste, were worth attending to, the Committee would do well to provide a few higher prizes in this section. The Sewing and Knitting done by the children in all the schools was pronounced by the Judges to be excellent, and a large quantity of Kindergarten work had been produced by the infants in a way very creditable both to themselves and to their teachers. There could be no doubt that the changes made in the Schedule for this section since last year had acted as a great encouragement, each Standard now having its own prizes. But there was obviously one further improvement still needed: viz, to provide (if practicable) some competition for the boys in manual work, answering to the needlework of the girls. This was a matter which had for some time occupied the minds of educationists all over the country, and had been thought worthy of mention even by the Royal Commissioners. Children under seven years of age received some little training of hand and eye through the Kindergarten system, but after passing into the first Standard they had, as a general rule, no further instruction of this sort until they left school. Under the New Education Code an attempt would be made to supply this missing link by encouraging some kind of technical work in the schools; and it would be well worth the while of the Committee to consider whether they could do anything to stimulate an interest in the matter. The parishioners were much indebted to the officers of the Society for the trouble they had taken to make the Exhibition a success, especially to the Secretary, Mr. J.H. Dawson, and his Assistant Secretary Mr. H.Holmes, and to Messrs. G. F. Lee and S. J. Deeley, the Secretaries of the Sub-

Committees. In conclusion, it was very gratifying to be able to say that there had not been on this occasion the slightest ground for suspecting any attempt at unfairness in any part of the competition.

The Prizes, amounting in value to £34 15s 6d. were then distributed, and the meeting closed with a vote of thanks to the Chairman, proposed by Mr. A. Cockeram and seconded by Mr. J. K. Colman.

A short meeting of the Committee was then held, at which the usual complimentary payments were voted to Messrs. Jas. Smith and Sons, to Mr. Thomas of Chatsworth, and to Messrs, W. Wall and J. Dare of Stancliffe, for their effective decoration of the tent, with shrubs and flowering plants. A special prize was also voted to Mr. C. E. Dawson for the loan of his excellent model of the Stancliffe grounds.

The following is the Report, referred to above, as read by the Secretary.

The Second Exhibition since the revival of the Society was held on Tuesday, Aug. 26th, 1890.

A very heavy thunderstorm broke soon after the opening of the Show, and this no doubt prevented a great number of persons from attending; but, as it was, the attendance was quite equal to that on any previous occasion. 1,031 persons paid for admission at the gate, and 915 subscribers' and admission tickets were collected.

The total number of visitors must have been at least 2,000. The show was financially a success; but as the accounts are not closed at the time of going to press, details must be held over for a future issue.

This year the Committee made several additions to, and alterations in, the Schedule of Prizes to be competed for; the total amount of prize-money offered (exclusive of sports) being £42 10s. 6d., but they regret to state that of this sum only £34 15s 6d. is awarded in consequence of there being so few entries in the Industrial Section: in some subjects not a single entry was received. The Committee hope that as the objects of the Society get better understood the Industrial Section will attract more competition and will be productive of much good.

The Schedule of Prizes for next year will be issued as early as possible, and the Committee strongly recommend intending competitors at next year's show to make early application for the Schedules, so that their work may be undertaken during the winter months. The total number of entries in the Gardening Section was 348, being an increase of 70 on last ycar. The Judges were Mr. Owen Thomas, Chatsworth; Mr. John Dare, Stancliffe; Mr. Chas. Simmonds, Sydnope; and Mr. Albert White, Darley House; and they state that the quality of the vegetables exhibited was very good, notably amongst the potatoes and collections. This year the gardens were judged on July 21st, the Judges being Messrs. Owen Thomas, J. Dare, A. Smith, A. White, and J. H. Dawson; there were 19 entries, a great increase on any previous year. Some of the gardens were very good, the First Prize Garden receiving 118^1/$_2$ points out of a total of 128, and the Committee think that this portion of the Society's work has already done much good in encouraging systematic work.

In the Industrial Section there were 89 entries as against 93 last year; the work done was very good, and visitors to the Show manifested great interest in the articles exhibited. The Judges were:-

For Nos. 1 to 11 (Domestic Work) and 19 to 24 (Fancy Needlework), Mrs. Booth, Mrs. Potter, Mrs. Arrow Smith, Mrs. Deeley, and Mrs. Dawson.

For Nos. 12 to 18 (Artistic and Mechanical Work), Mr. Patteson and Mr. C. E. Dawson.

For Nos. 25 to 27 (Honey), Mr. Walker, High Peak, Cromford.

For Churchtown Scholars' Work, Miss Fogg, Mrs. Knowles, and Mrs. Robertson.

For Two Dales Scholars' work, Mrs. Atkinson, Mrs. Clay, and Mrs. H. Holmes.

For South Darley Scholars' Work, Mrs. Booth, Mrs. Colman, and Mrs. Jas. Shaw

The model of Stancliffe Hall and grounds, which was exhibited at last year's show, and which was, by the kind permission of Lady Whitworth, modelled and suryeyed by Mr. C. E. Dawsn, has been considerably enlarged, and was again exhibited, and attracted a great deal of attention.

This year a small programme of Athletic Sports was arranged, and these were supplemented by various entertaining competitions kindly provided by Lady Whitworth.

The members of the Darley Dale and Rowsley Ambulance Classes gave two demonstrations of their work on the grounds, under the direction of Dr. W. Moxon and Police-constable Baker, and they were witnessed by a great number of people.

The best thanks of the Committee are due to His Grace the Duke of Devonshire, to Lady Whitworth, to Messrs. James Smith and Sons, to the Rev. F. Atkinson, to B. L. Harrow, Esq, A. Clay, Esq., and others, for the loan of valuable and interesting collections of plants and fruits. Also, to Lady Whitworth for the use of Stancliffe Park for the Show and for her handsome subscription; to the executors of the late Sir Jos. Whitworth, Bart., and other honorary members for their subscriptions to the Society; to the Judges in the several departments of the exhibition: to Mr. Walker for lecturing in the Bee Tent; and to the Derbyshire Bee-Keepers' Association for the loan of their tent.

[N.B. – The Committee hope to issue the Schedule for next year's show on as early a date as practicable, so as to enable intending Competitors in the Industrial Section to prepare during the coming winter. It is requested that any suggestions of alterations or additions to the Schedule be made to the Secretary, in writing, not later than Oct. 11th.]

THE NEW INSTITUTE

[We are requested by Mr J.H. Dawson, Secreary of the Reading Room, to publish the following announcements.]

The Committee of the Reading Room have had to give up the rooms in Two Dales from Michaelmas. They are glad to announce that, through the good offices of the Devisees of the late Sir Joseph Whitworth, they have arranged to carry on all their operations during the winter in the New Building in the Matlock Road, which is to be henceforth known as *"The Darley Institute."*

HOSPITALS

Lady Whitworth's daughter from her first marriage, Mrs. Mary Higginbotham, founded the Glasgow Nursing Association in 1875. Mary and Lady Louisa Whitworth took a keen interest in the welfare of their employees and constructed a building suitable for their care and convalescence. The building is on the west side of Whitworth Road opposite Sir Joseph's kitchen gardens and became known as The Sanatorium. Two years after the death of Sir Joseph Whitworth, a hospital was built by 15 legatees including Lady Whitworth on land adjacent to the A6, one hundred and fifty metres south of the Hackney Lane junction.

The new hospital was described in the St. Helen's Church Magazine for July 1888. "At a meeting of the local Board on June 12th, Mr. Beaumont, architect, of Manchester, attended on behalf of the legatees of the late Sir Joseph Whitworth to discuss the question of water supply to the new Cottage Hospital which is about to be built by Lady Whitworth and her co-legatees (Mr. Chancellor Christie and Mr. Darbishire) on a plot of ground fronting the high road between Darley and Matlock. The hospital is intended for the use of the district, and will comprise a general hospital for six beds, with large sitting-room for convalescent patients, and rooms for Matron and Medical Officer.

In a separate building are two wards for two beds each, for infectious diseases, with Matron's and Medical Officer's rooms. In connection with this building there will be a disinfecting chamber conveniently situated for use, not only by the inmates of the hospital, but also by anyone in the district requiring to have clothes, bedding, or any other property disinfected in the best and most effectual manner. Both the buildings will be very complete with all modern conveniences. There will be a lodge and entrance gates on the front or lower road, and also an entrance from the higher road. The contract has been let to Messrs. Southern and Sons of Salford, and the work will be commenced immediately." Two years later the magazine had this piece, on Lady Whitworth's rules for the hospital -

"By request we reprint the following notices which have already been published in former numbers of the Magazine.

Lady Whitworth and her co-legatees of the late Sir Joseph Whitworth are anxious that the people of Darley and the neighbourhood should know that the beds in the Hospital are for the use of any sick person who is certified by any doctor as being a suitable case for admission. No infectious case is admitted, but accidents or urgent cases are taken in at any time. The time of admission in ordinary cases is from 2 to 4 p.m. Patients can be visited by their Friends on Sundays, Wednesdays and Fridays, from 2:30 to 4 p.m.

N.B. In case of necessity, permission can be obtained from the Doctor to visit at any time.

Not more than two visitors will be admitted in one day.

Patients must come provided with comb and brush, and towel, a pair of slippers, some pocket handkerchiefs, and two night-dresses or night-shirts.

No article of food must be given to patients without the permission of the Matron or nurse. It is strictly forbidden to bring any intoxicating liquors into the hospital. Anyone breaking this rule will not be permitted to visit again.

A stretcher is kept at the hospital, and can be had on application for carrying patients or for cases of accident."

A maternity department was opened in 1989, taking over the service previously provided at Darley Hall, which had been converted to a maternity hospital in 1947. The Whitworth has a wide range of facilities for out patients, but has no resident doctor, and surgical operations once carried out there are now referred to the major hospitals at Chesterfield, Sheffield and Derby. Darley Hall is now a private residential home.

The Derbyshire County Council built a new sheltered housing complex at Chesterfield Road, Two Dales, called Underhall. The Derbyshire Dales District Council has another sheltered housing facility, consisting of wardened flats, called Broad Meadow at the bottom of the Oker Avenue estate. Adjacent to Underhall is a purpose built group surgery, and a dispensing chemist now occupies the former Westminster Bank across the B5057 opposite Underhall. Ivonbrook on the B5057 in South Darley, formerly the site of a saw-mill and Derbyshire County Council offices is now a residential home. There are two more residential homes on the A6 near the Hooley Estate area, Valley Lodge and Long Meadow.

EDUCATION

Darley Churchtown School was the oldest seat of learning in the area, and is recorded as having a school in 1627. Across the road from the main entrance to St. Helen's Church and just north of the old Rectory there is a building which also used to serve as a school room. The gable end of this building has a Latin inscription set into it.

The present Churchtown school dates from 1848 and was extended in 1911 and 1933 to its present size. The next nearest school northwards was over the Derwent in Great Rowsley about two miles away. There was formerly a National School at Two Dales on the B5057, which later became the Hayes Bakehouse.

Darley Churchtown School 1908

Owing to the large increase in the population of Darley Dale in the early twentieth century Greenaway Lane Council School was built in 1913. Before this new school relieved the pressure for school places the Whitworth Institute and the Methodist Chapel adjacent to the Blacksmiths Inn were brought into use. After the opening of the Greenaway Lane school the National School was only used for domestic science and woodwork teaching. Because of further expansion of the population after the Second World War a new school was built in 1952 adjacent to Greenaway Lane School as a secondary modern and the old school reverted to being a primary school.

Ten years later a large comprehensive school was built on the South Park adjoining the Broad Walk and Parkway housing estate area. This Darley comprehensive school was called the John Turner School as a tribute to Alderman Turner, a railwayman from Northwood Lane who had devoted a large part of his life to public office. This modern high tech school with all its facilities was, however, short lived, going out of use under Derbyshire County Council's school improvement plan which concentrated the over eleven education at a new school on Matlock Moor, three miles away, thereby ending secondary education in Darley Dale. Children over the age of eleven are now transported to school at either Lady Manners School, Bakewell, 6 miles away, or to Matlock. After the opening of the new comprehensive school at Matlock

Latin inscription on the old curate's house opposite St Helen's Church.
Believed to have been used as a school room in the 1700s. The inscriptions interpret as
'Keep from me the evil eye'.

John Turner School and Playing Fields 1960s

*The Whitworth Institute was used as a school 1912/13
until the Greenaway Lane School was built*

WHITWORTH INSTITUTE & GROUNDS DARLEY DALE

143

EXTRACTS FROM THE LOG BOOK

DARLEY DALE TEMPORARY COUNCIL SCHOOL

Oct. 1st 1908. Opened in what is now Hayes Bakery with one teacher Miss C. Blagshaw. 39 children on roll. Sometimes called the 'Anglican school'. Chesterfield Road, Two Dales.

Jan. 11th 1909. Miss C.J. Ault as headmistress opened a school after Christmas with 40 children on roll in the 1827 Chapel (in what is now Lewis Jackson Builders Store). Two Dales.

March 24th 1909. Mr. Anthony, of the 'National School' Churchtown visited to examine those children who were due to transfer at 8 years of age on April1st (the beginning of the new school year). The two school rooms in Two Dales appear to have been for infant age children who then completed their education to 12 years at Churchtown School.

Jan.8th 1912. The Darley Council School, mixed and infant departments. Arthur H. Child as headmaster opened the school in temporary accommodation in the Whitworth Institute. Miss Cockeram was in charge of infants. Number on roll, mixed 8-12 years old 108, infants 62, total roll 170. Miss Ethel Wagstaffe and Miss May Gill complete the staff of four. The other two schoolrooms appear to have closed at this point.

DARLEY DALE COUNCIL SCHOOL

May 19th 1913. School re-opened after the Whitsuntide Holiday in the permanent Council School building on Greenaway Lane.

July 25th.1913 Mr. Hand HMI and Mr. Widdows architect visited the school

Aug. 31st 1914 An Infants Department established as a separate school in the village calling itself the North Darley Council School, Infant Department. Miss C. I. Cockerham in charge.

Mar. 23rd 1915. Mr.Potts, County Inspector, visited to discuss the proposed occupation of the school by the military.

Mar. 23rd 1915. Head teacher attended the funeral of a late scholar killed on the railway.

Nov. 11th 1915. The head teacher now secretary to the recruiting committee with Lord Derby's scheme. Absent on several occasions.

June 1st 1916. An egg collection was made for the wounded soldiers at the Institute. A collection was also made for 'Our Soldiers over the Sea'.

Nov. 6th 1916. School closed for the winter months to conform to the 'Lighting Regulations'.

Feb. 5th 1917. A War Savings Association was opened in the school.

May 31st 1918. 'War Gardening Lessons' are being taken with Class 1 and 2 boys.

March 13th to 21st 1918. School closed to permit the staff to write out rationing cards.

Oct.17th 1919. Autumn Mid. Term holiday referred to as 'Peace Holiday'.

Jan. 5th 1920. The separate Infant Department closed and brought back into the main school.

South Darley School 2001

(Highfields) the John Turner School became an annexe to the Derbyshire County Council's Museum service. In the 1990s the former school and its large playing fields were sold off by the County Council to a developer, who demolished the school and built a housing estate on the site.

Evening classes and educational facilities were provided at the Two Dales Reading Room from 1849 to 1890, and have been provided at the Whitworth Institute from 1890 and Wensley Reading Room from 1891 to the present time. Most churches and chapels also ran Sunday Schools and the County Council also ran evening classes on a wide variety of subjects at the John Turner, Greenaway Lane and South Darley schools.

South Darley C. of E. village school was opened on 14th February 1860. Before that date children from South Darley went to Churchtown school. The 1860 school cost £356-15-4d. It still has its original bell which was restored in 1989 and is rung morning and afternoon to summon the children to classes. It is a small school with between fifty and sixty children on the register.

Stancliffe Hall scholars 1900s

Stancliffe Hall scholars 1900s

The tombs of Sir Joseph Whitworth, the second Lady Whitworth,
her daughter and step-daughter

The plain stone topped grave is that of the first Lady Whitworth
in the Ankers family plot at Tarvin in Cheshire

In loving memory of

Mary Louisa,

Widow of Sir Joseph Whitworth, Bart.

of Stancliffe, Matlock,

who entered into rest on the

26th May, 1896,

and was interred in the

Family Vault at

Darley Dale Church the

30th May.

The burial book of Lady Whitworth

The burial book of Sir Joseph Whitworth

In remembrance of

Sir Joseph Whitworth Baronet,

who died on the 22nd ulto, aged 83 years, and was

this day interred at Darley Dale Church, Derbyshire.

Stancliffe Hall, 2nd February 1887.

Stancliffe Hall 1880s showing the Winter Garden

Kitchen garden staff 1880s

151

Until recently there were two private schools in Darley Dale, Stancliffe Hall, closed in July 2001, and St. Elphins, still in existence.

STANCLIFFE HALL SCHOOL

In 1898, two years after the death of Lady Whitworth of Stancliffe Hall, the Reverend Ernest Owen from Llandaff Cathedral Choir School started his own school at the Hall, taking as the school motto the Latin phrase "In auspice numine" – In the Hands of God, or Beneath Gods Protection. The first pupils were twenty boys from the Choir School. These founder pupils were known as 'The Migrants'. Over the next one hundred years the imposing hall and its beautiful grounds resounded to the happy voices of hundreds of young boys and girls, no doubt to the delight of Sir Joseph's spirit. Sir Joseph was a great advocate of education and the Whitworth Hall at Manchester University is named after him.

The first headmaster built the beautiful wooden cedar chapel, which arrived in 1903, packed in crates, from Sweden. At that time the boys wore knickerbockers, and boxing and shooting were serious sports. Since then the school gradually expanded its facilities, a dormitory block in 1910, swimming pool in 1939, classroom block in 1967, school hall in 1972 (opened by the Duke of Devonshire), a preparatory department in 1978, a science, computer and art block in 1991 (opened by the Duchess) and a design and technology block opened in 1990.

Old boys of the '30s helped to dig the swimming pool, and hundreds learned to play golf on the nine hole course. Extensive playing fields catered for cricket, rugby, hockey, soccer, netball and tennis. Over forty years ago the school was organised as Patrols and scouting was very important.

This was replaced by outdoor pursuits, when agile youngsters learned to climb on the indoor climbing wall, as well as orienteering around the grounds and woods, canoeing and camping expeditions to the Hebrides.

By the summer of 1940, sixty-four Old Stancliffians were serving in the Forces and eventually they saw action around the world. They became Battle of Britain pilots, sub-mariners, tank commanders in the desert, leading regiments up the Normandy beaches, keeping open the Burma Road. Some became Admirals and Generals, one an Air Marshall and Commander-in-Chief of the Royal Indian Air Force. Over forty old boys gave their lives in the fight for freedom.

Two outstanding old boys were Midshipman Basil Guy, who won the Victoria Cross in the China War at the age of eighteen, and the D.S.O. in the 1914-18 conflict. The other was General Sir John Glubb (Glubb Pasha), founder and Commander of the Arab Legion in Jordan.

For the first seventy years the school was all boarding boys aged 8 to 13. Thirty years ago day boys began to appear, and some years later the first girls. There were seven headmasters in the school's history.

Boys and girls who went to Stancliffe Hall School now live in all parts of the world, and will remember Darley Dale as being a part of their younger days .

St Elphin's School

1844 was a momentous year in Warrington, Lancashire. Horace Powys, Rector of St. Elphins Church, founded a girls school so that women could benefit from a full and comprehensive education. The school was based at one of the oldest building in Warrington, the Old Priory, dating back to the twelfth century and surrounded by a moat. It was formerly a monastery and then a Convent. The phrase "Nisi dominus frustra" was adopted as the new school's motto – "unless we act in the name of the Lord we act in vain".

The Warrington school was known as the Clergy Daughters School. The building proved to be too old and unsuitable for young people, also unhealthy, and in 1904, sixty years afer its inception, it was decided to move the school to a more salubrious building.

At this time the Darley Dale Hydro was for sale. It was visited and found to be ideal, set in fifty acres, very accessible by road and rail, with its own farm and stables. An exploratory visit was made by the whole of the school, seventy girls plus staff, in the summer of 1904 prior to the move to Darley. It was decided to open the school to lay pupils and rename it St. Elphins School. The decision to move proved to be a great success.

A timber and corrugated sheet building was erected for use as a chapel. 1916 saw the stables converted into a permanent chapel, dedicated by the Bishop of Southwell, Bishop Hoskins. In the 1914-18 war the soldiers who were occupying the Whitworth Institute attended a play put on by the girls. Great scenes of jubilation attended the Armistice on 11th November 1918, with singing and cheering. The girls and staff at that time were without a cook, and had hardly any domestic staff so there were many extra chores for the girls to carry out.

In the following eighty years St. Elphins saw many changes take place in its curriculum and administration. The school grew from its original seventy girl boarders to approximately two hundred and fifty day and boarding pupils. It also now has a nursery department. The school has extensive sports facilities.

St. Elphins pupils come from many overseas countries and some old girls became very distinguished. The author of the Just William books, Richmal Crompton, was an 'old girl' and spent her youth at Darley Dale.

RELIGION

Chapels and churches in the North and South parishes of Darley Dale, pre-1982 boundaries

First Meeting Houses
North Darley, Orchard Cottage, Moor Lane, Hillside
South Darley, Greenstile Cottage, The Square, Wensley

1	Two Dales	Builder's store	1827
2	Wensley		1829
3	Hackney	Joiner's shop	1848
4	Oker	Dwelling	1851
5	Northwood	Demolished	1864

6	Deeley Town	Garage	189?
7	Farley		1901
8	Dale Road		1902
9	Hackney		1908
10	Rowsley		1910
11	Hillside		1912
12	Deeley Town		1928

St. Helen's	(Tower 1301)	900
St. Mary's		1845
St. Phillip & St. James	(Roof 1963)	1913
The Toleration Act – Nonconformism legal		1689
Dissentient Methodists founded the new connection away from the Wesleyans. They broke from the Wesleyans because of laymen being excluded from Conference		1797
Primitive Methodists broke away because the Wesleyans banned open-air meetings		1807
Repeal of Test and Corporation Act		1828
Congregational Union of England and Wales		1832
Marriages allowed in chapels		1836
Laymen's rights recognition		1877
Burials allowed with any or no service		1880

The first Methodist meetings at South Darley were held in Greenstile Cottage, fifty metres down the lane from Wensley Square. The first meeting of the Methodists in North Darley are believed to have taken place in Orchard House, situated at the junction of Gill Lane and Moor Lane, Darley Hillside. The house is dated 1786 and was the property of William and Bertha Gill.

1. The first Methodist chapel was built at Two Dales 1827 next door to the Blacksmiths Inn on the B5057. The date stone was removed in 1953 and built into the Dale Road Methodist Church Hall when it was constructed. The 1827 chapel has been used as a bakehouse and is now

a builders' store.

2. Wensley Chapel was built in 1829 on the B5057, one hundred metres above Wensley Square. The Local Preachers Mutual Aid Association was founded here by Frances Pearson in 1849 and is still thriving.

3. Hackney Chapel at the junction of Greenaway Lane and Grove Lane was built in 1848, went out of use in 1923 and became a joiners' and undertakers' workshop, powered by a gas engine. The Sunday School to this chapel was across the road, and has been demolished.

4. Oker Chapel, South Darley was built in 1851. It went out of use and became a house in 1994.

5. Northwood Lumb Lane Chapel was constructed in 1864, was a Mr. Squires' bakehouse between 1912 the late 1930s, and is now demolished.

6. Deeley Town Chapel adjacent to and just south of the Unity Complex was built in the 1890s and disposed of in 1928. It is now used as a service garage for Matlock Transport.

7. Farley Chapel at the junction of Farley Hill and Smedley Street West, Matlock, was built in 1901 and is still in use. This part of Smedley Street was in Darley Dale parish until recent times.

8. Dale Road Chapel on the A6 at the north end of the Whitworth Park was constructed in 1902 and has its own grave-yard. The adjacent Church Hall was constructed in 1953.

9. Hackney Chapel on Greenaway Lane was built to replace the 1848 chapel nearby.

10. Little Rowsley Chapel was built in 1910 on Chatsworth Road, which was in Darley Dale parish until 1980.

11. Darley Hillside Chapel was constructed in 1912 to replace the Lumb Lane Chapel, and was extended in the 1950s.

12. A second Deeley Town Chapel on the A6, opposite Firth Rixson, was built in 1928 to replace the first.

Methodist Meeting House, Greenstile Cottage, Wensley. Pre 1829

Orchard Cottage Meeting House, Moor Lane. Pre 1864 Primitive Methodist

Chapel 1. 1827 Two Dales Wesleyan, now a builder's store.
Date stone removed to Dale Road Methodist Church Hall

Chapel 2. 1829 Wensley

Chapel 3. 1848 Hackney Primitive Methodist Chapel, now a joiner's shop

Chapel 4. 1851 Oker Chapel, South Darley

Chapel 5. 1894 Northwood Lumb Lane Primitive Methodist. Now demolished

Chapel 6. 1890s Deeley Town Wesleyan Reform. Now a garage

Chapel 7. 1901 Farley Congregational, Smedley Street East

Chapel 8. 1902 Dale Road North

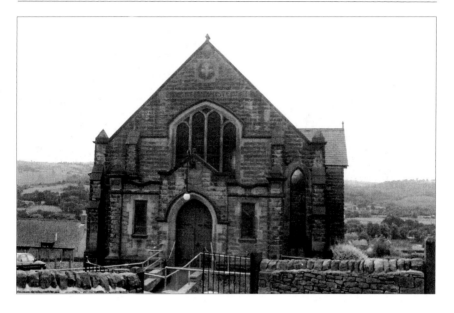

Chapel 9. 1908 Hackney Primitive Methodist replacing 1848 Chapel

Chapel 10. 1910 Chatsworth Road Rowsley

Chapel 11. 1912 Darley Hillside Primitive Methodists, Moor Road. Replacement for 1864 Lumb Lane

Chapel 12. Deeley town, Dale Road North, Wesleyan Reform. 1928 replacement for 1890s.

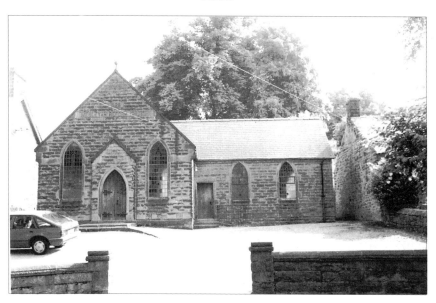

1903 Stancliffe Hall Chapel, private

Interior of St Elphin's Chapel 1950s

Hackney Sunday School, now demolished

Hackney Sunday School

Two Dales Chapel Sunday School 1900s

Darley Hillside Sunday School 1912

Two Dales Sunday School with banner

Darley hillside choir (above) in the mid 1950s. Back row from left to right; Mr JH Fearn, Mr A Vardy, Miss M Needham, Mrs L Draper, Mrs F Forbes, Mr K Wardman, Mrs E Wigley, Mrs Lomas, Mr H Wardman, Mrs N Gladwin, Mrs Bland, Mr JS Billingham, Mr H Gladwin, Mr A Wigley, Mr G Wardman, Middle row: Mrs J Lomas, Mrs L Taylor, Miss C Jefford, Miss M Greatorex, Mrs I Greatorex, Miss G Wardman, (?), Mrs M Wardman. Front row: Miss P Lomas, Miss J Wardman, Miss H Taylor, Mr P Vardy, Miss J Large, Miss M Draper

Hillside ladies' concert 1976. Back row left to right: Mrs I Greatorex, Mrs CM Billingham, Mrs M Vardy, Mrs L Draper. Middle row: Mrs M Wardman, Mrs G Barton, Mrs W Baugh, Mrs D Large, Miss J Large, Mrs M Loeber, Mrs P Taylor, Mrs L Taylor, Mrs S Berry, Mrs J Gibbs. Front row: Mrs J Woodhouse, Mrs B Hayward.

ST. MARY'S CHURCH, SOUTH DARLEY

St. Mary's was opened in 1845 after taking five years to construct, built in the Norman style under the supervision of the architect Joseph Mitchell of Sheffield. In 1863 its gallery was removed. The doorway to it can still be seen in the tower. In 1885 the east wall was removed and the chancel built to the design of Mitchell's son. This made spaces for another forty seats. The church has several unusual features. Its axis is more north/south than the usual east/west. The tower houses a carillon and its main window is reputed to be by Burne Jones.

St Mary's Church with clock, South Darley 2001

Sunday School scholars at St Mary's Church, South Darley. No clock

St Philip and St James Church, Hackney

CHORISTERS' 173 YEARS

Interesting Record of Three Darley Church Members

Left to right: **Mr. Wall, the Rector, Mr. Smith and Mr. Pilkington.**

The three members of Darley Parish Church choir shown in company with the Rector (Rev. W. F. Martin) possess an interesting record of service. Between them they have sung in the Darley choir for 173 years. Mr. Walter Wall, on the left, who is now 78 years of age, joined the choir in 1871, and has served continuously during the 68 years which have elapsed since that date. Mr. A. W. Smith was admitted a chorister in 1888, and he subsequently became a sidesman of the church and honorary lay reader. Mr. G. W. Pilkington became a chorister in 1885. The record is truly a remarkable one, and is believed to be unparalleled in the Church of England.

ST. HELEN'S CHURCH

The main church in Darley Dale is dedicated to St. Helen, whose saint's day is 18th August. She is reputed to have been the mother of the Roman Emperor Constantine, and to have lived at York. The church's origins are believed to date to the tenth century.

The church is built on a small ridge of land in the centre of Darley Valley floor, which extends through the present Churchtown school as

171

far as the site of the original Darley Hall (1066), now Abbey House. A very old yew tree grows near the church, approximately thirty-five feet in circumference. The Domesday Book (1086) states that Darley had a Church and a priest. In 1905 a portion of a Saxon cross was found in the churchyard. The cross, which resembles the Saxon crosses at Bakewell and Eyam, was removed to Weston Park Museum at Sheffield. One of the crosses in Bakewell churchyard was found on the

The four periods of architecture

St Helen's Church

Darley/Beeley Moor. Another stone believed to be part of a Saxon cross is built into the external wall between the porch and the tower. The smaller font is Norman, the decorated one is Jacobean Gothic. The church contains many varieties of architectural styles. The south side, near the side door contains four styles of architecture side by side, Norman, early English, decorated and perpendicular. The tower was built in the early 1300s. Other major alterations took place in 1885. In the porch are several sepulchral stones and outside are several old stone coffins. Guides to the building are available on request in the Church.

ST. HELEN'S REGISTERS

The old Register Books of St. Helen's Church, now in the Derbyshire Record Office, at Matlock, make most interesting reading. Some of the names mentioned are still common in the area, dating from the 16th century, such as (with different spellings) Ragge, Pidcock, Barker, Taylor, Stone, Lummas, Allen, Dunne, Stevenson, Vicars, Wall, Wiliamott, Needham, Roose, Wilgoose, Else, Daken, Milner, Holland, Bagshawe. Many strange christian names occur in the Registers, e.g. (male) Aberbatha, Seaward, Mordecai, Archelaus, Mihill, Porphyriman, Ottiwell, Jethro, Zebulon, Prince-John, Hemor; (female) Vina, Bathesheba, Bethia, Thomazin, Tabitha, Easter, Scythe, Benedicta, Walburge, Olinda, Faith, Troth, Silence, Patience, Prudence, Cristean, Damorish, Luce. In the late 1700s there was a surge of such names as Jemmy, Jenny, Molly, Billy, Sally, Nanny, Dolly,

St Helen's. One of the earliest register books

Becky, Peggy, Kitty, Betty, Nelly.

The cause of death was often given. Accidents and suicides are prominent and deaths of lead miners and beggars are common. Comments on exceptional weather were also noted. The first entry is dated 1539.

An entry in the burials dated 15th July 1685 is very sad, and a testimony to the very hard life lived by some. "A poor wandering girl aged about 10 died at Bridgetown" (now called Darley Bridge). A surprising number of men died at work in the local lead mines, and by inclement weather. Village folk-lore passed down the generations connects a house in Wensley Square with Snitterton Hall. Its windows are reputed to be glazed with glass bullions left from the glazing of Snitterton Hall. Glass for glazing in medieval times was made by rapidly spinning a large blob of glass. The glass near the perimeter was thin and reasonably clear. Only small pieces could be obtained and these were set into a lead framework, hence the origin of leaded lights. The centre bullions were discarded. A sure way of telling if glass is old is to look for circular lines in it. I noticed that one bullion at Wensley had scratched on the glass two names entwined, Susanah Renshaw and John Hacket, 1769. In 1766 Banns for the marriage of John Hacket to a Dorothy Simson were forbidden by a mother. John Hacket and Dorothy did not take long to find other partners, Dorothy marrying John Wilgoose in 1768 and, according to the inscription, John Hacket finding a new love, Susanah Renshaw, in 1769.

The Act requiring the keeping of Registers was passed on 29th September 1538. St. Helen's Church records are in the Derbyshire County Council Records Office at Malock, and are a mine of information on the original Darley Dale families. Here are some of them.

House in Wensley Square believed to be the original Trogues Farm with inscribed glass bullion 1769

BURIALS

1539	10th February	Henrie Stafford buried a child
1551	5th – 10th July	9 persons buried of sweating sickness Clemens Wall was amongs these.

It is interesting to record that the great-great-great-great-great-great-great-great-great-grandson of Clemens Wall occupied, until his death in December 1949, an important place in the church life of the parish.

1557	1st March	Agnes Buxton, died of plague
1558	14th April	Alice Stafford and five others, plague
1559	3rd February	Elizabeth Pendleton
	12th February	Agnes Ballidon
1560	January	Elizabeth Ballidon
1562	4th December	John Rowsley had a child buried
1581	25th May	Richard Needham
1589	14th July	James Plato
1590	14th March	Mr. Holland
1593	2nd April	Hugh Brough
1594	5th April	Mr. Vavesour
	14th April	Old Ottewell Williamot had a son buried
1612	1st October	William Carlell, a strange beggar
1616	15th December	John Warde perished with cold on the moor
1623	18th November	Joan Evans, daughter of parson of Darley
1624	25th January	Richard Baall
1631	3rd February	Ould Catharaine
1634	18th June	William Norman Robert Evans, parson
1640	31st March	John Supper
1642	6th June	Widdow Cheethome
1644	2nd April	Mrs. Walburge Columbell of Stancliffe

1644	29th June	James Holland, rector
1644	11th July	Margery Marshall of Rowsley-hall
1645	23rd February	Richard Bendbow
1645	4th March	An unbaptized son of Ottiwell Beeless
1645	13th September	Elizabeth Gregory, drowned in flood
1647	7th December	Collumbell, s. Mr. Fs. Grantham
1648	15th January	Charles Broxholme, rector
1648	13th September	Male child of Robert Gregory, drowned
1648	31st December	Thomas Frith, aged 106
1649	2nd February	James Tatersall, a stranger
1650	4th May	Ottiwell Arnfeild, a slater
1654	11th September	Ffrances, wife of Sir William Boothby, Baronet, aged 21. (Lady Boothby was the daughter of Col. John Millward of Snitterton. Her infant son Francis was baptized next day in Darley Church, 12th September)
1657	28th May	Damorish Buxton
1659	7th December	Edward Shackerlie
1662	11th June	Walburge Potte, Rector
1663	3rd December	Robert Dum
	20th June	Edward Paine, Minister
1665	11th July	Mary Paine, his widow
1669	30th July	William Hopkinson and Robert Sidwell (suffocated by firedamp in a mine)
1669	4th October	Captain John Milward of Snitterton
1670	21st September	John Milward of Snitterton, Royalist Colonel, M.P.
1671	10th April	Thomas Ironfeild
1673	8th July	Denis Hodgkinson (suffocated by firedamp in a mine)
1673	19th August	A maid from Snitterton Hall

1676	5th February	Roger Ball, killed in a mine
1676	8th May	Philipe Barnes, huntsman to Earl of Rutland
1676	12th September	A son of Abill, stranger, a Tinker
1678	30th May	Anne Giles, stranger
1678	17th June	Frances Chadderton
1685	24th Febuary	Thomas Moseley, Rector of the north Medyaty of Dearly
1685	15th July	A poor wandering girl from Lancashire about 10 years old, who died at Bridgetown
1687	February 22nd	Mr. William Bradley, schoolmaster of Darley
1688	December 18	Jane, wife of William Taylor of Oaker end, being lost on Oaker in a stormy night and found dead in the morning
1689	October 10th	Ann, wife of John Bestall, Wensley, who fell from her horse in the way to Chesterfield and died on ye moor
1689	December 16th	Mr. John Edwards Parson of Darley
1691	April 16th	Son of William Bateman, killed by a fall into a grove
1692	July 15th	Troth Wall, vid. of Wensley was buried
1697	December 6th	Richard Milner, Clerk of Darley
1700	February 29th	Peter Heward, Hackney lane, a Quaker, buried at Buntingfield
1701	January 30th	George Salt, a stranger, perish'd in the snow at Sandyford upon ye East Moore
1703	October 8th	Jane, daughter of Godfrey Taylor, drown'd in a well
1704	June 30th	John Wildgoose, kill'd in the Milnclose groove

1705	August 23rd	William Slack, of Wirksworth, a poor travelling pedlar
1705	October 30th	Frances Pidcock, vid. of the Lane
1706	April 18th	Mary, wife of George Hally ith Dale
1706	December 21st	Emund Parkin, killed in a grove
1707	July 5th	Henry, son of Henry Knowles, who was drowned in the River Derwent
1708	September 18th	John Clark, of Bridgetown, and Robert Tissington, of Ashover, both drowned in the Yalestoon groove
1710	April 7th	John Adams, commonly called Cowley John
1710	July 223rd	John Treviss, of Little Rowsley, killd by a tree rowling on him
1711	Sept 23rd	Samuel Guill, kill'd by a fall from a scaffold
1716	October 22nd	Alice Hoson, virg., Toadhole
1718	July 13th	ffrancis, son of John Tayler the Smelter
1720	January 26th	Robert Hawksworth, a youth
1720	October 5th	Mr. Henry Aldriche, Rector of Darley
1723	February 12th	Andrew Heath, late Schoolmaster of Darley
1723	December 3rd	James, son of James Dunn, who was murthered by his father
1733	February 19th	William Godwyn, aged 102 years (See tombstone in Churchyard)
1741	March 11th	Rev. William Beighton, Curate of Darley
1741	April 6th	Anne Taylor, found dead in Northwood
1742	January 21st	Jane Cutler, a travelling woman, died in Hackney Lane
1742	June 9th	Ann Knowles, Okerside, found in the River Derwent, lost December 24th before

1744	May 5th	The Rev. John Garmston, A.M. (formerly Fellow of Magdalen College in Cambridge), Rector of Darley and Prebend of the Church in Wolverhampton
1750	April 20th	Thomas Parkes (made a will never provd. Mr. Fern's Son-in-Law joint executor)
1751	May 22nd	Richard Jonts, an Exiseman
1753	March lst	Mary Wem Hospital child
1756	August 26th	Frances, wife of John Dakeyn, Toadhole Bank
1760	April 11th	A stranger unknown
1763	May 25th	Edward Swinscot, pauper
1764	April 29th	The Rev. Thomas Savage, Rector of this parish of Darley, A.M., and formerly fellow of New College, in Oxford (See Tablet in Church)
1764	December 6th	Joseph Cotterel, of smallpox, Hackney Lane (Many deaths from smallpox are recorded)
1770	January 14th	John Kidd, a discharged soldier
1773	April lst	Jane Milner, Deputy-Clerk or Sexton, a singular woman (See gravestone under East Window of Chancel)
1778	March 15th	Eliz. Dau. of Joseph Else, from another parish
1795	October 27	Jane Ball, killed with the fall of her house in bed
	November 5th to January 17th	
1799		Four daughters of John and Mary Fantem, Cowley Hall (See gravestone in Churchyard)

1800	November 25th	Samuel Holmes, drowned in Darwent at Matlock
1801	July 20th	Thomas Gregory, drowned himself, aged [sic]
1804	August 18th	William Holme, 46, drowned in Darwent at Matlock Bath
1805	August 18th	Joseph Adams, kill'd in a mine, him and another, and also another almost kill'd same time
1805	August 25th	George Holme, the same that was kill'd nearly above
1806	November 11th	Hannah, wife of John Gregory, son of Thos. Gregory, Clerk (she died after a long illness, November 8th at 3 o'clock ith morning)
1807	August 11th	Anthony Allen died suddenly gething a kit of Water to his Head
1808	August 18th	The Revd. Sir Willam Ulithorn Wray, Bart., Rector of Darley, Born Aug. 25th, 1721, and died Aug. 9th, 1808. He came to be Rector 26th Ap. 1764, and enjoyed the place upwards of 44 years (See tablet in Chancel)
1810	November 22nd	James Massey, an American Loyalist, aged 80 years
1811	October 21st	Thomas White, killed by the falling of an arch of a bridge near Uttoxeter
1812	November 23rd	Mary, daur. of Robert Mason, of Northwood, burnt to death
1814	May 11	Frances, daur. of Wm. Dunn, by drinking oil of vitriol
1814	September 20th	John Kirkland, a suicide, found hanging in Little Rowsley Meadow

1817	June 20th	Jacob Flint, drowned in attempting to catch a piece of wood in the Derwent
1818	January 26th	Rev. Edward Jones, late Curate of this Parish, aged 73 (See gravestone under East Window)
1819	February 14th	Francis Bowler, 28, drowned in Mr. Dackeyne's dam
1824	February 26th	Rachael Tomlinson, 54, a lunatic, drowned herself in the Derwent
1824	November 10th	George Thacker, Toadhole, 13, run over by a cart
1825	February 19th	John Lees, 21, drowned below Darley Bridge on Sunday Evening. He had just left the publick-house

(See gravestone in churchyard which has the following verse inscribed on it

How melancholy was the news
To those I loved so dear,
To hear my precious life was gone,
Assistance none was near.
Repent with speed, make no delay,
I, in my prime, was called away)

1825	April 27th	James Barnes, killed by a fall of stone in the Dalefield mine
1826	November 4th	Thomas Gregory, Parish Clerk and Schoolmaster, aged 93
1827	December 15th	Abel Wragg, killed in a stone quarry on Beeley Moor
1830	June 26th	Benjamin Stone, Wensley, 51, died suddenly by the visitation of God
1831	February 4th	Charles Down, aged 1 year, died in consequence of drinking boiling water from the spout of a kettle

1835	May 6th	Elizabeth and Sarah Vickers, Wensley, sisters aged 26 and 13, buried in the same grave
1836	July 19th	Elizabeth Hardy, 64 destroyed herself by burning, being insane
1842	June 1st	John Young, Toadhole, Infant, drowned in a trough
1842	August 10th	Marg. Holmes, Torside, aged 58, drowned herself in the Derwent
1843	May 26th	William Shaw, Cross Green, 16, killed by a heavy Coal falling on his chest
1846	March 29th	Hannah Haynes, Wensley, 67, burnt to death
1846	October 10th	Robert Clayton, Holloway, 19, Charles Clayton, Holloway, 17, 2 brothers, buried in one grave

From 1847 to 1881 the majority of the entries record in a marginal note the causes of death which vary from the ordinary ailments such as "Consumption, Dropsy, Bronchitis," etc., to the more tragic ones of "Dropped down dead," "Killed in a drunken fight" and so forth. One of the last in 1881 records an unusual time for Burial. It is marked "Small Pox, buried at 1.15 a.m."

CHURCH OF ST. PHILLIP AND ST. JAMES, HACKNEY.

This was constructed in 1913 to supplement St. Helen's Church. It was renovated and altered in the early 1960s, with a new roof clad with wood shingles.

VILLAGE HALLS

Joseph Taylor, a native of Wensley, who went into the brewery business (Eagle Breweries, Manchester), became a benefactor of South Darley

183

and Wensley. In the early 1890s he had built fifteen good quality terraced houses in Wensley, Eagle and Oker Terraces, to be let to local families at a rent of two shillings and six pence (12^1/$_2$p) per week. These are now privately owned. On his death he willed them to his daughter Lady Roberts who sold them to Mr. Tom Wright of Warney Lea House (now the Dales and Peaks Hotel) opposite the A6/Greenaway Lane junction in the 1920s. In 1891 Joseph Taylor also built the Wensley Reading Room and gave it to the parish. It is still in use. He provided a new wing to the school and a new east window in the Church.

What was understood to be the best village hall in the County was provided by the legatees of Sir Joseph Whitworth for the use of the people of Darley Dale and district. The Whitworth Institute and its park have been the centre of village life for central Darley Dale for over a century.

After the Second World War several village halls were built. The Northwood Institute at the junction of Northwood Lane and the Cote Hillock road to Tinkersley was built by subscription in the 1950s. It later became a night club and was later sold for private use. South Darley also built a new village hall next to the school in the 1950s, still in regular

South Darley Village Hall built 1952

use. These village halls were of concrete prefabricated construction. In the 1980s a new village hall/community centre was erected by Darley Dale Town Council to serve the needs of the southern end of the parish. This is situated on the Darley Dale/Matlock boundary on the A6 opposite the iron railway bridge over the Derwent.

Little Rowsley's leisure needs were met by Great Rowsley's village hall just over the Derwent near the school. They also use Great Rowsley's recreation ground nearby.

As mentioned previously the first recreation hall in Darley Dale was the Reading Room at Two Dales.

CHAPTER 5

THE ECONOMY OF THE VALLEY

From prehistoric times to the late 1700s Darley valley was, like neighbouring villages, primarily based on agriculture. However on the west side of the valley there had been a lead mining industry since Roman times. This area was close to, or part of, the Roman lead mining field known as Lutudarum. Since mediaeval times mining in the area was administered by Barmote Courts, in both the High Peak and Low Peak. Barmote Courts are believed to have come into being in the late 800s under the Danish Courts in the Wirksworth area, which was part of the Danelaw. Wirksworth Hundred's old name is the Soke and Wapentake of Wirksworth, soke and wapentake both Danish words meaning an administrative area.

The Barmote Courts which administer the lead mining laws are reputed to be among the oldest industrial courts in the world. Lead mining laws are reviewed periodically. The first recorded review was at Ashbourne in 1288. To bring the lead mining laws within common law two more Acts of Parliament were passed, in 1851 for the High Peak and in 1852 for the Low Peak.

By 1748 the London Lead Company had a Newcomen steam engine working on lead veins in the South Darley/Winster area. The lead mining industry continued in operation on the west side of the valley until the closing of Millclose Mine in 1939. The lead smelting works associated with Millclose, and still in operation, recycling lead, were moved to the Millclose site in the early 1930s from Lea. Such was the

𝔜ou are hereby required to attend the GREAT

BARMOTE COURT, at The Carriage House, Chatsworth

for the liberties of ASHFORD, TIDESWELL, PEAK

FOREST, HARTINGTON, STONEY MIDDLETON

& EYAM, in the County of Derby.......................

.... not later than 12 noon ....

.... on Wednesday ....

.... the 7th day of November 2001 ...

& later, at the Carriage House Restaurant, Chatsworth

𝔅ated this 30th day of September 2001 ....

W.M. Erskine Barmaster.

To *L R Jackson Esq.*

𝔜𝔬𝔲 𝔞𝔯𝔢 𝔥𝔢𝔯𝔢𝔟𝔶 𝔯𝔢𝔮𝔲𝔦𝔯𝔢𝔡   to attend

the GREAT BARMOTE COURT, at the MOOT

HALL, within the Soke and Wapentake of

Wirksworth, in the County of Derby....................

.... not later than 12 noon ....

.... on Wednesday ....

... the 18th day of April 2001 ....

𝔇𝔞𝔱𝔢𝔡   this 12th day of March 2001   ....

W.M. Erskine   Barmaster.

To   *L R Jackson Esq.*

quantity of lead being extracted around this period that the smelter based at Lea could not cope. Between four hundred and five hundred thousand tons of lead ore, galena, was won from the Millclose Mines complex. The mine and smelter in the mid 1930s employed approximately seven hundred men.

The railways around the same time employed about six hundred. Stancliffe Estates, including the stone company, employed about two hundred and eighty men & various heavy haulage firms a similar number. Johnson's Ladygrove corn mill, formerly Dakeynes flax mill, provided employment from the 1780s and is still operating, unlike Johnson's Old Road corn mill. The Old Road corn mill was twice the home of the Bakelite Company, from the early 1920s to 1927/8 when the firm outgrew Darley Dale and moved to Birmingham. Part of Bakelite moved back to Darley Dale for the duration of the Second World War.

The nursery industry, including James Smith & Sons, has been in Darley since 1827. The Smith nursery has been a large employer of labour. It is is recorded in St. Helens Parish Magazine for October 1890 that James Smith & Sons entertained all their employees at the Nags Head (now demolished) and the Plough Inn, Two Dales, a total of one hundred and fifty men and boys. It always struck me as odd that so many men in Darley with limited education could fluently reel off the Latin plant and plant species names, and spell them with no trouble. James Smith & Sons ceased trading in the 1980s after over one hundred and fifty years. They had over two hundred and fifty acres of land under nursery cultivation at their peak in the early 1900s.

After the Second World War the Derbyshire County Council headquarters moved from Derby to Matlock, providing more employment for the people of Darley Dale and district.

There were also two precast concrete works in Darley district, one established in 1950 at Warren Carr, Cowley, and the other in 1923 at the Stancliffe Stone quarry.

Darley Dale has maintained a good economic outlook over the past two hundred years. Undoubtedly the high note of this prolonged economic boom was the coming of the railway in 1848 and the availability of the London to Carlisle trunk road from the mid 1800s. These, together with the abundant supply in the valley of lead and stone, ensured prosperity. The Great Depression of the period between 1929 and 1939 did not affect Darley Dale badly because of its four prosperous and stable industries – railways, lead mining, quarrying and the nurseries.

BANKS

Banking in Darley Dale began with Dakeyne's Bank of Darley at Holt House, Two Dales. In St. Helen's Church magazine of March 1893 there is reference to the Whitworth Institute Savings Bank, which was open on Tuesday evenings between 6 and 8 p.m, and paid interest at three per cent per annum. Mr. Joseph Henry Dawson was appointed agent and accountant to the Bank. The Institute building also housed the Bank of Sheffield and Rotherham. Regulations for the Whitworth Institute Savings Bank in 1893 read

"Deposits will be received at the Institute every Tuesday Evening, between 6 and 8 p.m. Each Depositor will receive a Book of Account, and must produce it whenever money is paid in or withdrawn. Money may be withdrawn at any time after notice (on a Form to be had at the

counter), given in on one Tuesday for the next. The Governors will allow interest at the rate of Three per cent. The Governors have appointed Mr. Joseph Henry Dawson their Accountant and Agent in this business, who will receive and pay, or arrange for the receipt and payment, on their behalf.

Signed, for Lady Whitworth, Mr. Chancellor Christie and self,

R.D. Darbishire"

The London County Westminster and Parr's Bank announced on 29 July 1920 that they were opening a new branch at Darley Dale, attached to the Matlock branch. The hours of business were to be daily 10-3, Saturdays 9.30-12. The first premises were in a temporary hut. The bank paid £125 for a plot of land and £650-15-2d for the hut. Permanent offices were built at a cost of £1693 and were completed in 1924. In 1923 the bank had changed its name to the Westminster Bank. In 1968 Westminster Bank and the National Provincial Bank, along with

The first bank at the junction of A6 and B5057 Two Dales road 1920

Replacement for the first bank

National Provincial's subsidiary District Bank, announced their intention to merge. The operations of all three banks were combined over the following 18 months and they began to trade as National Westminster Bank from 1 January 1970.

The first free standing bank occupied the site, later occupied until 2000 by the Westminster Bank. This was a small, stout, wood and corrugated iron clad structure. When it became redundant, with the building of a permanent bank on the site, it was moved to James Smith & Sons head office site on Park Lane, where it served as an office until 1974, when it was moved again to Wheatley House, where it still stands. The Sheffield Bank moved into a permanent building across the B5057. It was taken over by William & Glyns, and then the Royal Bank of Scotland. The Derwent Valley Cooperative Society also had a savings bank in each of their four branches in Darley and district, at Little Rowsley, Northwood and Central Darley on the A6 and at Two Dales.

AGRICULTURE

Farming and leadmining were the staple industries of the valley from Roman times. There are still many traces of medieval ploughing on the west side of the valley. Burley Fields farm was mentioned in the Domesday Book, along with ploughs and bee keeping. The original 1066 Darley family were associated with horses. 1,600 acres of land in North Darley had been enclosed prior to the Enclosure Act of 1764. A further 2,417 acres, approximately four square miles, of common land were enclosed under the Act. In 1831 257 families totalling 1,266 people resided in North Darley. 96 of the families were mainly employed in agriculture. 302 of the population were male, 21 years of age and above and of these 123 (40%) were employed in agriculture. It is interesting to note that the average household was composed of approximately five people.

Two annual fairs for the sale of cattle and sheep were held at Darley Flash, at the place now known as Moor Farm. Moor Farm also served as an Inn. The fairs were held on the 13th May and 27th August. Darley Wakes Week with a travelling fair took place at Darley Bridge on the area between the Square and Compass and the river Derwent. This was held around 18th Augusty to coincide with St.Helen's saint's day.

In the 1862 White's Directory for Sheffield and twenty miles around, the combined acreage for North and South Darley was given as 7,004 acres (approximately 11 square miles) with a combined population of 2,202. South Darley's population was 582, in an area of 2,004 acres (approximately 3 square miles) with 28 farmers, 3 wheelwrights and 1 blacksmith. North Darley's population was 1,620, and its extent was 4,999 acres (approximately 8 square mile), with 30 farmers, 7 wheelwrights and joiners, 3 blacksmiths and 1 cattle dealer – George Shaw.

Bulmer's Directory of 1895 gives a combined acreage of 7,103, with a combined population of 2,933. South Darley covered 2,008 acres, with a population of 754, which included 21 farmers, 1 cow keeper and 1 wheelwright. North Darley's area was 5,095 acres, its population totalling 2,179, including 22 farmers and 3 blacksmiths.

The farmers listed by Bulmer in North Darley were Joseph Allen,

Christopher Allsop and Jonathan Barker of White Springs; Henry Bowler, Farley; James Buckley, Cockshead; George Carnell, Ash Tree Farm; Thomas Evans, Northwood; Thomas Fearn, Tinkersley; William Ford, Burley Fields; George Gregory, Tor Farm; William Gregory senior, Morledge Farm; William Gregory junior, Hackney Lane; Devereaux Hall, Tinkersley; Samuel Redfearn, Darley Moor; Daniel Wagstaff, Mill Road; Mrs. Ann Wall, Fallinge Farm; George Wall, Tinkersley; Mrs. Hannah Wall, Hall Farm; John Waterfall Tax Farm; Fred Wildgoose, Farley; Herbert Wragg, Farley; Richard Wilson, Bumper Castle. In South Darley there were Herbert Carline; Adam Clay senior; Adam Clay junior; Arthur Cook, Snitterton Hall; John Derbyshire; Edward Fawley; John Greatorex, Oker; William Hardy, Gurdale; William Hadfield; John Haynes, Oker; Joseph Hill, Bridge; Joseph Marsden, Oker; William Mountney, Leawood Farm; George Page, Oker; Joseph Potter (and ground bailiff), Mill Close Mine; James Meakin Sheldon, Tiersal; William Stevenson, Oker; Joseph Francis Smedley, Brightgate; William Taylor (farm bailiff), Cowley Hall; Mrs. Maria Twigg; Francis Young, Oker.

Sir Joseph Whitworth built a completely new Model Farm at the junction of the A6 and Whitworth Road in the 1870s. This included stabling, cow houses, granary, vehicle and farm machinery storage areas, and farm manager's house. Upon the death of Lady Whitworth in 1896 Stancliffe Estates Ltd. turned the farm buildings into their offices and stone works. Whitworth had the old Tor Farm demolished and its remains can still be seen adjacent to the pre-1831 A6 north/south highway. These are located across the present A6, opposite Holmesfield, Dale Road North. A new Tor Farm was constructed at what is now the south end of Firth Rixons. The new Tor Farm was also demolished in the year 2000.

Many farms have gone out of use in our valley. Horses, the mainstay of agriculture for over a thousand years, disappeared in a relatively short time, beginning with the First World War of 1914 to 1918, which took a heavy toll of the horse population of Britain. Tractors and specialised farm machinery made steady progress up to the Second World War. After the second war the farm horse finally vanished from use. Farm horses and many farm workers were superceded by machinery. Two shire horses did the farm work at Hall Farm at the rear of Darley Hall up to the 1960s. I believe this farm never had a tractor. Hall Farm no longer exists as a farm.

INDUSTRY

Lead mining was confined to the limestone country on the western slopes of the valley. The lead industry was intensified in the mid 1700s by the London Lead Company and existed up to 1938/9, when the largest lead mine in Europe, Millclose, closed. Seven hundred men were employed in total by the mine and its smelter.

The Nursery industry was very active on the north east side of Darley. The largest of the nurseries was James Smith & Sons, founded in 1827 and occupying at the time of the First World War approximately 250 acres, and employing 150 staff who were highly skilled in all matters horticultural.

Birmingham Town Hall, constructed from Stancliffe stone 1910/12

St George's Hall, Liverpool. Constructed from Stancliffe stone

Technical Institute and Library, Liverpool

Stancliffe 1912

Stancliffe masons

Stancliffe masonry

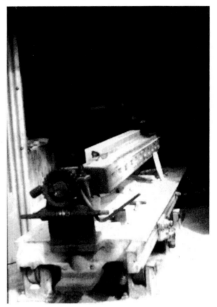

Planing machinery

Stancliffe Yard 1912

Stancliffe works in its last days

Stonework in steps, cornices, and doorways, in the grand hall, Chatsworth, carried out in Stancliffe stone in 1912

Stancliffe yard 1970s. Brian Richards, Les Holmes, Edward Holland

Large block of stone in Stancliffe Quarry 1912

Stancliffe Quarry 1912

Stancliffe Quarry 1912

Stancliffe Quarry

Stancliffe Quarry

Stancliffe Pre-cast Stone.
Wrestling with the casting box. Left to right: Jim Taylor, Reg Street, Jack Clyne, ?,
John Porter, Colin Hunt. Statues of 'Verona Fathers' for St Teresa's Church, Sheffield

Stripping the casting box for the statues of the Verona Fathers. Gerry Smith, MD, left and Jim Taylor, right

Gritstone quarrying was carried out along the eastern side of the valley. There were quarries at Fallinge in Little Rowsley, Lumb and Bent lanes at Darley Hillside, Hall Dale and Knabb quarries north and south of Two Dales, quarries on Holt Road Hackney Road, and Farley. The largest was Stancliffe Quarry. The quarry and masons' yard employed over two hundred men. Stancliffe Quarry dates back to antiquity and Darley Dale's St. Helen's Church was built of its stone around the first millennium. The tower was added in 1301, also constructed from Stancliffe stone. On the north slope of the valley above Little Rowsley there was a large gritstone quarry, Fallinge Quarry, now disused. In the vicinity was an old lead smelt, hence the name Smelting Wood Brook.

Two Dales had a large flax mill, built around 1780s by the Dakeyne family. This very substantial building is situated on and powered by

STANCLIFFE ESTATES LTD.

Some of the Time Sheets for week ending 15th March 1928, divided into sections – Quarry, Works, Railway, Garage, Nurseries, Engineers and Joiners.

The total wage cost; for the week was £774.15s.6d. and included crusher men, artificial stone 'Precast' men, lorry drivers and storeman, for whom I have neither time sheets or names. The totals are after deductions for rent; contributions etc. I believe around 285 men were employed by the Company at that; time.

Hall Dale Quarry was being worked. Stancliffe Estates owned considerable property, and had a large building section to keep it in repair and carry out building works.

Approximate men and boys figures.

Works	90
Both Quarries	123
Crusher	13
Artificial stone Precast	16
Engineer/Blacksmith	8
Garage	2
Lorries	4
Railway men	5
Nurseries	7
Stores	
Joiners	16

My brother Jim, born 1912 and still active, is on the Nursery time sheet earning the princely sum of 16s.6d. (82^1/2p) for 49^1/2 hours work.

Jim Taylor of Peakland View, Darley Dale, who worked at Stancliffe from 1956 to 1973, kindly lent me these 73 years old time sheets, which he had the forethought to rescue many years ago. Jim is son-in-law of Jack Hallows of Cherry Tree Farm, Darley Hillside, whose grandfather Joseph Hallows is mentioned on the 1847 and the 1855 Sale Notices of the old Stancliffe Estate.

Jack Hallows' mother and my mother worked together in Stancliffe Quarry, along with several other women in the First World War when they were twenty to thirty years old.

The Stancliffe Quarry is now owned by the author. Nearing the end of its life the quarry is still in production today 2001.

Stancliffe Estates, the Precast stone yard, and the sawing and masoning yard are now only a memory.

Listed below are the names of people who worked for Stancliffe from the 1950s to 1977. The list supplied to me by Jim Taylor and Reg Street is by no means comprehensive. Apologies for any omissions or wrong name spelling. Several names were in the 1928 wages sheet.

1928 wage sheet

No.	NAME	Hrs.	Rate	Amount
84	Thos. Turner	45	2	6 10½
85	Chas. Bark	47¾	2	11 6½
86	Thos. H. Boam	47½	2	11 6½
87	John. Dodd			
88	Chas. P. box	46½	2	11 6½
89	John. Maddox	49¾	2	4 6½
90	Ronald. Allsop	48½	2	10. 6.
91	Ben. Gregory	44	2	5 10
92	Edw. Daniels	47½	2	11 6½
93	F. Hutchinson	34	1	15.5.
94	Fred Gregory			
95	John. Downs	48	2	10.0.
96	James. Webster	48½	2	10.6.
97	J.H. Baswell	48½	2	10.6.
98	G. Maper	48	2	10.0.
99	Walter Fawley	48	2	10.0.
100	Chas. Kirk	40½	2	2 2.
101	Cyril. Taylor	47½	2	11 6½
102	J.H. Townbrow	49	2	11 0½
103	H. Knowles	40½ 1/4½	2	15 8
104	Robert. Clarke	48¾ 10	2	1 3
105	J.H. Whitehead	47¾ 6½	2	11 6½
106	Roger. Wilson	49 1¼	2	15 1½
107	John. Taylor	52	2	18 6
108	Thos. Boam	47½ 10	2	1 3
109	John. Gill	55 ½	2	19 7
110	J.F. Downs	48½ 1½	2	6 5½
				298 15 4½

Gerrard Smith, M.D.

Office Staff
Dennis Fearn
Reg Boden
Audrey Redford
Elizabeth Wilson
Una Kreibich
Margaret, Wright:
Pauline Hallows
Natalie Atkin
Christine Boswell
Daryl Yates

Draughtsmen
Harry Tideswell
Roy Marsden

Junior
Draughtsmen
Michael Herman
Keith Wathall

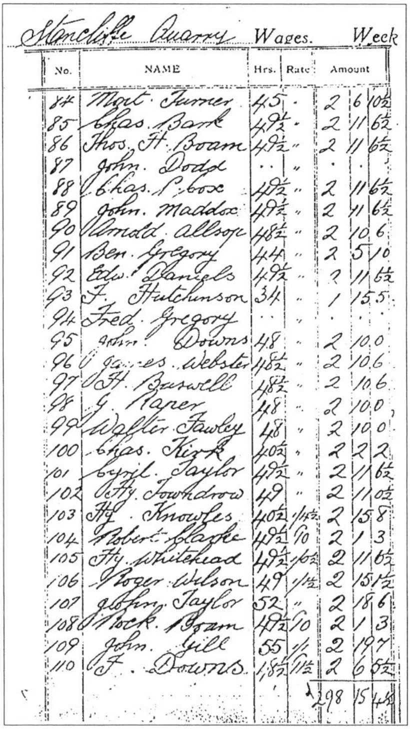

Masons
Ernie Harlow
Harry Bailey
Frank Brown
Brian Williams

Wallstone
Sid Quigley

Yard
Foreman Roy
Everett
Les Holmes
Charlie Slaney
Ray Housley
Don Willers
John Smith
Harold Cundy
Trevor Lancaster
David Thorpe

Saws
Stan Willers
W. Thornhill
Ken Barwick

Carborundum Saw
Fred Ollerenshaw
'Tink' Whelbourne

Stone Planes
Rex Marsden
Herbert Wragg
Eddie Holland
Cyril Howes

Blacksmiths
Pat Devaney
Dick Wilson

Garage
Billy Bell
Bill Wayne

Crane Drivers
Graham Sellors
Edgar Pashley
George Draper

Quarry
Foreman Bill
Needham
Bill Elliot;
Albert Downs
Jack Goodwin
John Noton
Billy Wilson

Crusher
Joe Allwood
Ron Marshall

Canteen Ladies
Bernice Casey
Gladys Crowder

Precast.-1956
onwards
Foreman Eric
Richards
Brian Richards
Reg Street
Tommy Coe
Jim Taylor
Dick Peach
John Pritty
Geoff Pritty
Brian Bent;
Bernard Cooper
John Taylor
David Taylor
Peter Stone
Brian Crookes
John Porter
Ernie Knighton
Colin Hunt

Doug Goodall

Mixers
Jack Ayre
Tommy Rhodes

Joiners
Henry Fearn
John Jackson

Stancliffe Quarry Wages. Week 15.3.28.

No.	NAME	Hrs.	Rate	Amount		
·	Chas. S. Gill	wk.		5	·	·
1	G. Charlesworth	49½	1/5½	3	12	2
2	G. Norman	52	"	3	15	10
3	Thos. Holland	44½	1/4½	3	1	2
4	Thos. Allwood	49½	"	3	8	0½
5	Walter Walters	49	"	3	7	4½
6	John Hallam	40	"	2	15	0
7	Wm. Taylor	··	"	·		
8	Elias Morten	49½	"	3	8	0½
9	J. S. Carter	52	"	3	11	6
10	J. G. Knowles	42½	"	2	18	5
11	Jos. Debanks	49	"	3	7	4½
12	A. Billinge	22½	"	1	10	11
13	John Allsop	13½	"		18	6½
14	Reg. Wagstaffe	49½	"	3	8	0½
15	A. Halksworth	49½	"	3	8	0½
16	Arthur Boden	49½	"	3	8	0½
17	Jos. Barker	49½	"	3	8	0½
18	Edw. Turner	36	"	2	9	6
19	Jos. Allwood	49½	"	3	8	0½
20	Stan Grafton	49½	"	3	8	0½
21	Geo. Taylor	49	"	3	7	4½
22	Chas. F. Gill	49½	"	3	8	0½
23	James Wilson	45½	"	3	2	6½
24	Hedley Wilson	37½	"	2	11	6½
25	Thos H. Barker	··	"	·	·	·
26	Wm. Marsh	38½	"	2	12	11
27	Everard Chell	46	"	3	3	3
28	Walter Boam	49½	"	3	8	0½
29	Andrew Holmes	49½	"	3	8	0½
30	John Wyatt	40½	"	2	15	8
31	Thos. Wilson	56½	"	3	17	8
32	John Siddall	53	"	3	12	10½
33	Chas. Hallows	··	"	·	·	·
34	Ernest Cooper	21½	"	1	9	6½
35	F. Wagstaffe	49½	"	3	8	0½
36	E. Allwood	49½	"	3	8	0½
37	Sam. Grafton	40	1/4	2	13	4
38	James Fielding	17½	1/-	·	17	6
39	H. Camell	49½	1/4	3	6	0
40	Geo. Carter	49½	"	3	6	0
41	Ernest Smith	49½	"	3	6	0
42	Eric Acton	49½	"	3	6	0
43	Albert Downs	48½	1/3½	3	2	7½
44	James Grindey	48½	"	3	2	7½
45	R. H. Holland	49½	"	3	3	11
46	Hy. Buttler	40	"	2	11	8
47	John Bagshaw	48½	"	3	2	7½
48	Thos. Wildgoose	49	1/4	3	5	4
49	Thos. Hutchinson	34	1/3½	2	3	11
50	John Spencer	29½	"	1	18	1
51	John Maddox	53	"	3	8	5½
52	Jos. Lynam	49½	"	3	3	11
53	Dan. Wagstaffe	43	1/4	2	17	4
54	Jos. Allen	48½	1/3½	3	2	7½
55	Herbert Smith	49½	"	3	3	11
56	Wm. Needham	49	1/3½	3	3	3½
57	Chas. Waterfall	48½	"	3	2	7½
58	Frank Allsop	48½	1/2½	2	18	7
59	Lewis Flint	49½	"	2	19	9½
60	Law. Gould	48	"	2	18	0
61	Cecil Holmes	49½	"	2	19	9½
62	Jos. Allwood	49½	"	2	19	9½
63	John Woodhouse	71	"	4	5	9½
64	Jos. Wall	49½	"	2	19	9½
65	John Crossland	48½	"	2	18	7
66	Stan Willers	8½	1/0½	·	8	10
67	Robert Carding	40½	1/1½	2	5	6½
68	Alf. Wagstaffe	45	1/0½	2	6	10½
69	C. Morten	48½	1/1	2	12	6½
70	John Slater	49	"	2	13	1
71	James Newton	49½	1/0½	2	11	6½
72	Matt Stanley	49½	"	2	11	6½
73	Wm. Mason	50½	"	2	12	7
74	E. W. Arridge	50	"	2	12	1
75	A. Wagstaffe	49½	"	2	11	6½
76	Ernest Thompson	49½	"	2	11	6½
77	Geo. McNevin	43½	"	2	5	3½
78	Geo. Wood	49½	"	2	11	6½
79	Herbert White	49½	"	2	11	6½
80	Edgar Ashley	49½	"	2	11	6½
81	Arthur Carding	49½	"	2	11	6½
82	Geo. Holland	51½	"	2	13	7½
83	Sam. Wood	36	"	1	17	6

"Works" Wages. Week 15. 3. 28.

No.	NAME	Hrs.	Rate	Amount		
1	E. J. Warren	35	1/7½	2	16	10½
2	J. E. Harlow	44	"	3	11	6
3	G. Frost	44	"	3	11	6
4	J. Brooks	50⅝	"	4	2	8
5	W. Smith	44	"	3	11	6
6	H. Wragg	.	1/9	.	.	.
7	J. Robb	44	1/7½	3	11	6
8	F. Beaumont	24	"	1	19	0
9	A. Wagstaffe	50⅝	"	4	2	8
10	G. Kilner	7	"		11	4½
11	G. H. Brooks	32	"	2	12	0
12	F. Smith	44	"	3	11	6
13	S. Ollerenshaw	44	"	3	11	6
14	J. K. Bagshaw	49½	1/6½	3	16	3½
15	A. Frost	48	"	3	14	0
16	J. Raynor	47	"	3	12	5½
17	J. Hanson	49½	1/7½	4	0	5
18	Hy. Brooks	49½	1/6½	3	16	3½
19	J. Hancock	49½	1/0½	2 BARGAIN	11	6½
20	J. Twigg	49½	1/3	3	6	10½
21	F. Holmes	71½	1/1½	4 BARGAIN	0 6	5 0
22	A. Sheldon	63½	"	3	11	5
23	J. H. Smith	67½	1/4	4	10	0
24	S. Wagstaffe	67½	1/0½	3	10	3½
25	G. Wood	66¼	"	3	9	0
26	L. Riley	71½	"	3	14	5½
27	O. Booker	71½	"	3	14	5½
28	S. Zaker	71½	"	3	14	5½
29	Job. Charlesworth	62⅞	"	3	5	6
30	W. Thornhill	63½	"	3	6	1½
31	F. Cowley	71½	"	3	14	5½
32	J. Howe	49	1/4½	3	7	4½
33	R. Allsop	49½	"	3	8	0½
34	C. Halksworth	22	"	1	10	3
35	G. A. Wagstaffe	40½	"	2	15	8
36	G. Chell	47	"	3	4	7½
37	S. Barker	45½	"	3	2	6½
38	B. Cooke	53	1/4	3	10	8
39	Jos. Charlesworth	.	"	.	.	.
40	C. E. Hayto	56½	"	3	15	4
41	Hy. Hickman	62⅞	1/4½	4	6	5½
42	W. A. Atwood	62	"	4	5	3
43	B. Gregory	70	"	4	16	3
44	J. Waterfall	59½	"	4	1	9½
45	C. Bishton	49½	[illegible]	[illegible]	[illegible]	[illegible]
46	J. Hickman	[illegible]	[illegible]	[illegible]	[illegible]	[illegible]
47	[illegible]	[illegible]	[illegible]	[illegible]	[illegible]	[illegible]

No.	NAME	Hrs.	Rate	Amount		
				177	9	
58	B. Allsop	37½	1/0½	1	19	0½
59	J. Thraves	34½	"	1	15	11
60	D. Holmes	49½	"	2	11	6½
61	S. Wall	33	"	1	14	4½
62	J. Roberts	63½	"	3	6	1½
63	E. Daniels	48½	"	2	10	6
64	Hy. Lees	40½	10d	1	13	9
65	J. Wood	49½	1/0½	2	11	6½
66	D. Allsop	71½	"	3	14	5½
67	W. Wood	63½	7d	1	17	0½
68	G. Page	49½	9d	1	17	1½
69	J. Marsden	67½	5½d	1	10	11
70	C. Stancey	31	5d		12	11
71	G. Atwood	59½	4½d	1	2	3½
72	C. Cowley	19½	5d		8	0
73	J. Roose	44	9d	1	13	0
74	Hy. Hodge	43½	5d		18	1½
75	J. Wagstaffe	44	"		18	4
76	D. Wagstaffe	49½	1/4½	3	8	0½
77	W. Bunting	49½	"	3	8	0½
78	F. Bucklow	49	1/0½	2	11	0½
79	G. Wall	51⅜	1/4½	3	10	7½
80	R. Thraves	51⅜	"	3	10	7½
81	E. Smith	44	1/7½	3	11	6
82	A. Stafford	18	1/0½		18	9
83	A. Thaws	44	1/7½	3	11	6
84	W. Dickinson	49½	[illegible]		11	0
85	W. Slater	24	1/1½	1	5	0
	E. ~~[illegible]~~	24	"	1	5	0
	Geo. Smedley	49½	1/1½	2	15	8
	J. C. Hunter	16½	1/7	1	6	1½
	C. K. Boden	16½		3	10	
	R. Watts	16½			12	6
				245	19	5

Less Insurance. [illegible] A. Stafford

J. Hunter

March 15th 1928 Garage & Engineers Wages. Railway Nur

Engineers

No.	NAME	Hrs.	Rate	Amount		
1	C. W. Dakeyne	Wk	£5	5	0	0
2	W. Charlesworth	54½	1/7½	4	8	6½
3	R. White	71¾	1/6½	5	10	7
4	W. Whitehouse	71¾	1/4½	4	18	7½
5	J. Siddall	56¼	1/4½	3	17	4
6	W. Waterfall	48½	11½	2	6	5½
7	J. Charlesworth	65¾	1/4½	4	9	10½
8	W. Bell	49½	1/3½	3	16	3½
				£34	7	8½

Garage

No.	NAME	Hrs.	Rate	Amount		
	R. Whittaker	54½	1/3	3	8	1½
	A. Moody	58½	60/-	3	10	10½
	A. Wilmott	54½	9d	2	0	10½
	L. Saylor	42	3d		10	6
	N. Marsden	31½	1/-	1	11	6
	A. Marsden	37½	11d	1	14	4½
	J. Fletcher	49	11d	2	4	11
				£15	1	2

Railway

No.	NAME	Hrs.	Rate	Amount		
1	J. Geddes	69 1/16	1/4½	4	14	11½
2	A. Fawley	72 1/16	1/0½	3	15	1
3	A. Travis	49½	1/3	3	1	10½
4	J. White	48½	1/0½	2	10	6
5	M. Cropper	56½	1/4½	3	17	8
				£18	0	1

Nurseries

No.	NAME	Hrs.	Rate	Amount		
1	H. Wragg	49½	1/-	2	9	6
2	H. Fielding	49½	-	2	9	6
3	Joe Allsop	53⅜	1/1	2	17	6½
4	H. Fawley	49½	1/-	2	9	6
6	J. Jackson	49½	4½		16	6
7	J. Fielding	49½	1/-	2	9	6
8	Geo. Hennett	40½	1/-	2	-	6
				£15	12	6½

Joiners

No.	NAME	Hrs.	Rate	Amount		
1	H. W. Gregory	49½	1/6½	3	16	4
2	E. Blackwell	49½	1/2	2	17	9
3	E. Lane	46½	1/4	3	2	-
4	E. S. Walters	43	1/5	3	-	11
5	Joe Derbyshire	49½	1/4½	3	8	½
6	E. Travis	49½	6½	1	4	9
7	J. Brewster	49½	1/0½	2	11	6½
8	Hy. Fearn	[illegible]	[illegible]		12	-
10	J. S. Ayre	49½	1/4½	3	8	½
12	F. Wilson	45½	1/5	3	4	5½
13	G. Brown	49½	1/0½	2	11	6½
14	E. Haslam	49½	"	2	11	6½
15	G. H. S. Walters	49½	"	2	11	6½
	J. Siddall Junr.	49½	"	2	11	6½
				£37	12	-

Works	245	19	5
S. Quarry.	337	4	7½
Crusher.	31	15	6½
A. Stone Dept.	39	2	5
Engineers.	34	7	8½
Garage.	3	18	7½
Lorries.	11	2	6½
Railway.	18	0	1
Nurseries.	15	12	6½
Stores	2	11	6½
Joiners.	35	0	5½
	774	15	6

Ladygrove Brook and its system of dams, and probably employed around one hundred and fifty people.

A timber yard belonging to John Gregory & Sons on Old Road specialised in English hardwoods, supplying the cotton bobbin and other wood manufacturing industries.

There were many small businesses – grocers, shoe-makers, stone merchants, blacksmiths, rope makers, masons, builders and joiners, butchers, bakers and besom makers, and a corn and flour Mill at Warney Lea, Two Dales.

RAILWAYS

From 1848 to 1966 the railway played a very important part in the life and economic situation in Darley Dale, in its heyday employing over six hundred people. The old railway station (Paxtons) and goods yard, which was the terminus in 1849, was the forerunner of the railway associated industrialisation for this area.

The station designed by Paxton opened on 4th June 1849 complete with sidings. The line was extended northwards up the Wye valley instead of the original plan to proceed through the Derwent Valley. The first phase to Hassop opened on lst August 1862 and in 1877 the sidings and marshalling yard began to develop in the area from Derwent Lane to a point four hundred metres south of Rowsley Station.

In 1873 a pair of railway houses were erected on Derwent Lane adjacent to the level crossing known as Nannygoat crossing. Railway housing was also built at Chatsworth Road, Little Rowsley, commencing in 1871 with thirty-nine cottages and followed in 1886 with a further twenty-five, and in 1896 another thlrty-one. By the 1901 Census Little Rowsley, part of Darley, had one hundred and thirty-one dwellings with a population of six hundred and thirty-nine.

In the 1920s a new loco shed was constructed to the south of Nannygoat Crossing which held twenty-seven to thirty locos. The old loco sheds adjacent to Rowsley new station were demolished and the Express Dairy Company built a milk collection and distribution factory

Rowsley old yard. Foreground right – cattle loading bay. Milk collection lorries in front of Paxton's 1850 station. Goods depot in the background on the right.

Rowsley old yard 1920 before Express Dairy. A6 road bridge at right hand background

Rail track from Rowsley old yard looking south showing Express Dairy's water cooling tank

Unity Complex, Toft lorry 1976

on the site with rail milk tanker loading facilities.

After the closing of the railway in 1968 the Derbyshire Dales District Council purchased the rail track and Rowsley and Darley Stations. The Express Dairy site became an industrial estate. The Old Yard industries were demolished and the shopping complex named Peak Village, and a housing estate, were erected on the site in the 1990s. The presence of the railway at Little Rowsley led to a surge of industrialisation which continues today. Deeleys and Bodens ran stone masonry businesses in the Old Yard. There was also a livestock loading facility in the yard and sheep and cattle were transported from our area all over the country. The civil engineers Lehane, Mackenzie and Shand occupied part of the site from the 1940s to 1996 and K.S.R. refractory material manufacturers also had a factory there from the 1940s until the 1990s.

Several transport firms operated from this area. Shirley and Proctor and the Express Dairy Company both had fleets of lorries collecting milk from peakland farms for distribution by the Express Dairy milk depot. Some milk went by rail tanker to London attached to express trains. The land southward from the Express Dairy Depot, bounded by the A6 and the River Derwent as far as Nannygoat Crossing, became a huge marshalling yard, all ending with the closure of the line in 1966 under the Beeching Rail Rationalisation programme.

In the Second World War it was the policy of the government to relocate essential industries from cities to rural locations for safety. The steel stamping factory Firth Derihons of Sheffield was one such factory, moved to Darley Dale in 1940 The site was adjacent to the railway, the A6 and the River Derwent which provided an adequate water supply. The site was ideal. The local population was large enough to provide labour. The factory was built on the L.M.S Sports Ground. The general area near the factory was then called Deeley Town (1900 to 1950), named after the Deeley family who lived in the only large house nearby – Riversdale. Firth Derihon Stampings Ltd, now Firth Rixson, is still a thriving concern employing approximately 400 people in 2001

Situated between Northwood Lane junction with the A6 and the steel works on the west side there is a small industrial estate called the Unity

Toft Brothers started at Youlgrave with steam wagons. One of the drivers was called Marsden, always known as 'Steamer'. An early Toft Brothers and Tomlinson Foden steam wagon RA6170 Registered in 1928

The Norde gang (North Derbyshire Engineering). Left to right: G Davis, W Needham, L Jackson, S Foxlow, F Blair (driver), R Wragg (designer)

Left to right: Charles, Alf, Doris 'Mother', Richard Henry 'Father', Eric, George. The Lowe Transport family early days 1958
Richard Henry Lowe was the founder of Matlock Transport Ltd 1945. He was Toft Brothers transport manager through the Second World War. The job also included co-ordinating other local transport firms with the Ministry of Transport.

RH Lowe

Complex. This group of buildings was formerly the home of the transport firm of Toft and Tomlinson, established in Youlgrave after the First World War. They moved to this site in 1927 around the time of the completion of the railway engine shed close by. Toft and Tomlinson were in Darley from 1927 to about 1980. Matlock Transport (Lowe brothers) has also operated from the area between the Unity Complex and the steel factory since the 1980s. They have another yard at the junction of

James Wooliscroft

The Wooliscroft family in the early 1950s at Blackpool. Left to right: Selwyn, mother Nancy, Peter, Barbara and John on a Silver Service bus trip. Father James, who drove the bus, was having a nap on the return journey

Darley Dale cricket ground 1900s

Northwood Lane and Cote Hillock Lane (Tinkersley). Cote Hillock Lane was part of the original highway before the construction of the modern A6 in1829. Across the A6 from the Unity Complex Strutts Engineering factory manufactures hydraulic grabs.

Cobb Slater's plastics factory occupies a site on the west side of the A6 at its junction with Church Lane. This was originally built as a workmens hostel in the Second World War. It afterwards became all instrument works, and now specialises in injection plastic moulding. Behind the Grouse Inn, off Whitworth Road, is the old Stancliffe Estates yard, originally built as a model farm by Sir Joseph Whitworth to serve his estate. Stancliffe Estates used this as their masons' yard, loco engine shed, wood yard and blacksmiths shop. It was also home to several other small transport firms. They sold petrol and generated electricity from the 1920s. It is now owned by Molyneaux Engineering, which is based there along with a variety of other businesses.

Down Church Lane, just north of the railway line, on the site of the new Willow Road estate, was the Derwent Valley Water Board's pipe storage yard, full of huge steel pipe sections for servicing the Derwent Valley water pipe line. Over the rail crossing, and at the rear of the Church, were James Smith & Sons' willow nurseries which were coppiced each year for the manufacture of horticultural baskets.

Along Church Lane and turning right on to the B5057 the present day picnic site and car park (adjacent to the cricket ground) was the site of the Hide and Skin Company, whose building was demolished in the 1950s. Adjacent to the building was the terminus of the aerial flight overhead cable-way to the Millclose lead mine, now H.J. Enthoven & Sons smelting works.

Opposite the end of Church Lane is Old Road, which owing to the proximity of Darley Dale's own small railway sidings, became an industrial site. It has been the location for a coal yard and builders merchant (Thomas Smith & Sons), petroleum distribution centre (B.P), the Bakelite factory from 1923 to 1933 and 1940 to 1947, civil engineers (Lehane, Mackenzie & Shand) 1924 to 1947, a transport garage for the Silver Service Bus Company, Lowndes Haulage, John Gregory & Sons' wood yard and S & E Johnson's corn mill. Over the rail bridge on the left in the 1800s was Walton's flour mill, which became the birthplace of the D.F.S nationwide furniture company from the late 1960s, owned by the Hardy family. Proceeding onwards towards the A6, on the right is the Red House Equestrian Centre and Carriage Museum.

Crichton Porteous, author

Turning left at the junction with the A6 three hundred metres north at the junction with Warney Road stands the Texaco filling station and shop. This was built by the Toplis brothers in the early 1930s as a base for their haulage business. The adjacent Warney Road leads to the B5057. Straight across the junction is Park Lane. Three hundred metres up Park Lane was the site of James Smith & Sons Nursery headquarters and packing sheds, now the Porteous Close housing estate, built in 1977. This estate was named after the

The Cottage, home of the author, Crichton Porteous

Porteous Close, named after the author

famous Derbyshire author Crichton Porteous who lived at the junction of Park Lane and Wheatley Road from 1946 until his death in 1991.

The next turn right off Park Lane is Wheatley Road leading again to the B5057. Across the B5057 is Ladygrove Road leading to S & E Johnsons' mill, formerly Dakeyne's flax mill, built in the 1780s, and the three dams on the Ladygrove brook which powered the mill, and still helps power it today. Retracing your steps to the B5057 towards the A6, Twyford's builders yard was from the 1870s to 1936 at the rear of Hayes Bake-house – the old National School.

There were two more builders and joiners in the area, F.A. Gregory & Sons (from 1900), joiners and undertakers, at Warney Road, and Walter Bowler & Son at the junction of Greenaway Lane and Grove Lane, established in the 1850s, and now Lewis Jackson (Builders) Limited. There were two smithies in Two Dales, located at Park Lane and in the yard to the former Blacksmiths public house, which dates from 1633.

Crossing over the Derwent to the west valley slope the industry was historically agriculture and lead mining, with a sawmill at Ivonbrook, Eversleigh Rise (now a Nursing Home). Transport, lead smelting and a precast concrete works are now the principal industries.

CHAPTER 6

LOCAL FIRMS

SHANDS

Lehane, Mackenzie & Shand Ltd, usually called simply Shands by local people, was registered as a private company in September 1924. Robert Lehane, a builder and local quarry owner at Birchover founded the firm of R. Lehane & Company to carry out general building work,

Baslow bridge

specialising in stone work. This company built many houses, churches and other public buildings. Mr Basil Mackenzie was an eminent water engineer, responsible for many large water works undertakings. In 1912 he was engineer in charge for the Kinder Reservoir in the Peak District . Lt.Col. Shand was a construction engineer and worked on the Kinder Reservoir with Mackenzie. He undertook a contract for a pipe line in 1923 with Mackenzie, for which Lehane supplied the stonework. This undertaking was the origin of the Lehane, Mackenzie & Shand company.

Robert Lehane unfortunately died just before the company came into being, and his widow was made a director. Mackenzie was the chairman from 1924 until his death in 1936. Lt. Col. Shand was chairman from 1936 until his death in 1952.

The company's first undertaking was the new Baslow road bridge on the A6020. William Froggat of Darley was a mason-fixer on the job. The next contract was for the construction of the Brownhill reservoir for the Batley Corporation, a five year contract worth approximately £450,000. This was to be the first of several impounding reservoirs constructed by the company.

Two brothers, Major Meares DSO, MC, and Neville C.S. Meares became directors and ran the firm through the Second World War while Lt.Col. Shand was away on active service. Lehane, Mackenzie and Shand became one of the first companies to carry out open-cast coal mining on a large scale, in 1942. Shortly afterwards they opened another large open-cast mine at Asherfield which yielded an average of five thousand tons per week. After the war the company expanded into the construction of sea defences, flood alleviation and major road construction.

In 1958 a consortium was formed with the civil engineering contractors Cubitts and Fitzpatrick & Son, for very large civil engineering contracts and the construction of the new motorways. Lt. Col. Shand's son Alexander became a director in 1949 and chairman in 1954. Duncan Milliken, who joined them in 1941, became a director in 1954 and Managing Director in 1961.

Lehane and Shand. Left to right: Geoff Sellers, David Holmes, Ernest Fox, Les Walker

Several local employees of Robert Lehane stayed with the new company in 1924 and became its secretaries. Edward Lynam retired in 1939 and Francis Sydney Cooper in 1948. Henry Milner Fielding was appointed a Director in 1954 and retired in 1959. Frederick George Stevens succeeded F.S. Cooper as Secretary in 1948, retiring in 1957 after fifteen years service. Many other people joined the company's administrative staff at the head office at Normanhurst and settled locally – Duncan Milliken and George Roger Gascoyne, Secretary and Director respectively in 1954, Raymond Jeffrey Phillips, Estimator and Director in 1952, and Derek Ronald Price, Contract Manager and Director in 1961. Several families had two generations work for Lehane, Mackenzie & Shand and the Holmes family had three.

Fred (grandfather), David (father), and David (son) from the 1920s to 1987. Likewise the Fox family, George, Joe (transport manager) and David; other Foxes (no relation) Ernest, John and Stewart. Fletcher brothers, Ken, Alan, Neville and Jerry. Billy Goodwin, Brian Allwood,

Ernest Crowder, Geoff Barnsley, Les Walker, Jack Farley, Bill Barker, Jim Bradbury and Adrian Barber, just a few of the many local men who worked in the plant yard at Darley and Rowsley. Many more local men, including the author, worked at various times on civil engineering sites for the firm.

Lehane, Mackenzie & Shand's plant yard was at Old Road, Darley Dale, with a plant storage depot at Oddford Lane, now the site of Forest Nurseries. They outgrew the Old Road premises after the war and moved to the Old Station yard at Rowsley, where in the 1960s they employed over one hundred men. A new wooden office block was built in the early sixties in the grounds of Normanhurst, which the company purchased in 1953.

Local contracts included Baslow Bridge in 1924 (their first job), Fernilee Reservoir on the Buxton to Whaley Bridge road in the 1930s, Ogston Reservoir south of Chesterfield, Derby Storm Water Culverts three miles in length under the city, three contracts for the improvement of the Derwent Valley Water Board's forty-eight inch (1200mm) diameter steel water main totalling nineteen miles including the concrete pipe bridge over the Derwent arm of the Ladybower Reservoir. Some of these were through very steep and rough terrain.

They also had the contract to divert water from adjacent valleys to the Ladybower Dam, some two and a half miles of forty-two inch (1070 mm) and thirty inch (760mm) pipes, plus a tunnel. Lehane, Mackenzie & Shand also built the Firth Derihon Stampings factory on the A6 at Darley Dale in the early 1940s as part of the government's dispersal of production essential to the war effort. They carried out the Darley Dale sewerage scheme in 1961/3, Shipley Park open-cast coal site in the 1960s, and Heads of the Valley road scheme in the 1950s.

The Hymac, an American invention, is a hydraulic excavator for which Lehane Mackenzie & Shand acquired a manufacturing franchise. It was constructed for them at Rhymney by Powell Duffren, and they set up a company, Peter Hamilton Equipment Ltd, in Rowsley to market the machine. The Hymac was exported world wide, and Geoffrey Sellers, son of George Sellers, one of James Smith & Sons nursery men, became

Hymac's Service Engineer and travelled the world from Canada and Africa to China, servicing their machines.

In the 1960s the company shortened its name to Shand. Ken Dabell became successively plant manager, director and managing director. The firm ceased trading in 1987.

BAKELITE

The Bakelite firm, successively known as Mouldensite, Bakelite, Bakelite Xyonite and BP chemicals, was born during a visit to America by representatives of J. & P. Hill, Sheffield, makers of Furnace Bricks. Hills were offered an agreement with the Condensite Corporation to import their phenol/formaldehyde resins and moulding materials into the U.K. This subsequently led to the formation of a U.K. Company to handle sales (and subsequent manufacture) of Condensite materials. At a later stage the American Corporation was taken over by the Bakelite Corporation which also included the Redmanol Corporation, whose U.K. representatives were A.W. Bishop and L.T. Bishop. The outcome,

Bowl manufactured at Darley Dale in the 1920s

226

Old Road Industrial Estate left to right: Lowndes Transport, SE Johnson, formerly Bakelite site. Old Road was a continuation of the Cote Hillock, Derwent Lane, Church Lane, Rowsley to Matlock road pre 1831. The toll house stood where Old Road joins the A6

in the early 1920s, was the formation of Mouldensite Limited and all previous activity at Sheffield (including some of the employees) was transferred to a new site at Darley Dale, which now manufactured phenol/formaldehyde resins, moulding powders and mouldings.

In the mid-twenties (1926/27) further American activity culminated in Bakelite Limited being formed (including a Birmingham Company, the Damard Lacquer Co. Ltd., then primarily concerned with liquid products, including lacquer for brass bedsteads – then a thriving business). The major decision taken immediately was to concentrate all manufacture on a new 30 acre site at Tyseley, Birmingham. This was most successful and remained a major factor in the business up to and after the second world war, despite the introduction and growth of many other plastics materials and products.

Prior to the transfer of all manufacturing activities to Birmingham, the production of "Laminates" was introduced at Bakelite Corporation's suggestion, and proved to be a very satisfactory operation, the maximum useage being in the electrical and radio industries. The moulding of individual items, including bowls, door furniture etc., was introduced and later abandoned upon the pursuance of a policy of making and supplying materials only. Trade moulders catered for the general trade and large electrical and radio manufacturers installed their own moulding plants.

Bakelite returned to its Darley Dale site during the Second World War to produce materials used by the armaments industries, particularly laminates used in aircraft manufacture. The Mosquito fighter-bomber was designed around the capability of wood faced phenolic laminates to be the main body reinforcement. The Hengist and Horsa gliders were made on a similar basis. Most bomber and fighter planes had Bakelite insulation generally in addition to control panels. The Darley Dale factory certainly contributed to the war effort but regrettably could not be embodied into the overall subsequent enormous demand for a wide variety of plastics materials. Bakelite production is now based in India.

There was only one local member of the Bakelite staff who moved to London or Birmingham – George Slack, who went to Birmingham. One local employee who spent all his working life with the company, and ended at the top of it, was Percy Smith, now aged 83 and living in Canterbury. Mr. Smith was born in Darley Dale in 1910, opposite what was to be the site of the Firth Rixson factory. He was educated at Darley School, Churchtown and Lady Manners School, Bakewell, where because of family reasons he had to leave at the age of 15 before taking his County Scholarship. He started work at Darley Dale on 9th November 1925 at the age of 15. His wage was ten shillings per week (50p in today's money!). His job was office boy. Mr. Smith recalls that to compete he had to learn "how to learn" and how to apply himself to a wide variety of activities. He had much help from many of his colleagues both technically and commercially. When he retired twenty years ago he was Managing Director of the Bakelite Company.

STANCLIFFE, 1897-1947

Sir Joseph Whitworth acquired Stancliffe Hall and its estate about 1856. After his death in 1887, aged 84, the second Lady Whitworth continued to reside at the Hall and run the estate until her death in 1896. The future of the Hall and estate was then resolved by its purchase by a number of local business men, who in 1897 formed a Limited Company called Stancliffe Estates Limited. It was an innovative and progressive company. Darley Dale at that time was dominated by an immense gritstone outcrop north east of the A6, about four hundred yards north of Church Lane, The area had been turned into extensive rock gardens by Sir Joseph Whitworth. The new company decided to extract the high quality stone in a most spectacular way by connecting the quarry with the Midlands Railway Manchester to London main line, by means of a standard gauge rail track. Stancliffe had always been worked as a quarry. Darley Church tower was constructed from it in 1301, and in the 1780's the famous Crescent at Buxton. The stone for these buildings and others at that time were transported by the road and canal network of that era. With the arrival of the railway at Darley in 1848 a small siding was made opposite the Church Inn. From there Paxton, architect of the Crystal Palace, built to house The Great Exhibition of 1851, sent base stones from Stancliffe for some of the exhibits. Stancliffe Stone also forms the base of the Albert Memorial, and Trafalgar Square was paved with it.

The Stancliffe rail track ran from an east facing junction with the main line midway between Church Lane and Darley Station. The line passed by the recently erected Broad Meadow sheltered housing complex, then through what is now the Oker Avenue estate, before going through a tunnel under the A6 near Broad Walk recreation ground. The tunnel is still in use today as a pedestrian subway. The track then ran in a cutting (now filled in) behind Peakland View, under a small footway bridge into the Stancliffe masonry yard, before proceeding west through Stancliffe yard buildings. These buildings were originally Sir Joseph's Model Farm. They are now Molyneaux Engineering Works. From here the line crossed Whitworth Road, passing along what is now

A6 tunnel Stancliffe railway. The first very small siding was in front of the Church Inn in what is now the Inn's car park. A branch line and private siding was established between Darley Station and Church Lane. The line ran through the area where the Oker Avenue Estate is today, then under the A6, now a subway

Cutting at rear of Peakland View and bridge for footpath to Whitworth Road and Stancliffe railway

Rail track through Stancliffe masons' yard looking towards Whitworth Road

Road tracks to quarry and crusher now part of Sir Joseph Lane. Stone crushing plant visible through the trees towards Whitworth Road

Rail track on A6 side of Stancliffe Quarry with high level branch line to quarry

High level bridge over cutting 1880s. Part of Sir Joseph's rock gardens and drive from the A6 to Stancliffe Hall

Stancliffe Quarry workmen and rail track at the cutting in the 1930s

The cutting as it is today 2001

Site of stop block end of Hall Dale loop at the junction of Whitworth Road and Moor Lane. The line ran to here from Stancliffe yard alongside Broad Walk estate then up to Hall Moor Road crosssing

Rail road looking west from Hall Moor Road crossing. War time Home Guard building on the right.

Rail track to Hall Dale Quarry and Hallmoor Road crossing

Rail track looking west in Hall Dale

Dawson's funeral, Green Lane

Sir Joseph's Lane towards the Stancliffe Quarry area. At the end of the lane the line split, the track to the left passing through the woods close to the north side of the A6 almost as far as the Firth Rixson factory. There was a siding and a junction in this area which took the line back into the quarry at high level. The track then went into a loop, and returned back towards Whitworth road, gaining more height in order to feed the huge quarry waste tips. From the end of Sir Joseph's Lane the rail track also carried straight on into the bottom of the quarry.

A third short branch from the split went back to the crusher and Precast Stone works. The engine sheds were located in the masonry yard area. Heading back east from the Stancliffe masonry yard towards the main line, the track passed under the previously mentioned small footbridge, where another junction to the left ascended a steep gradient between the recreation ground and South Park Estate. A very large quarry waste tip was formed in this area, which now forms the recreation ground area. Leaving the tip area the track continued up the hillside alongside the South Park estate, turning towards the west to arrive at a stop block near the junction of Whitworth Road and Moor Lane. A bungalow now stands on the site. Leaving the stop block the track headed east again on a down grade to a junction to the left. This enabled the engine and trucks to gather momentum for the steep incline up Darley Hillside towards Hall Moor Road, passing below the ruins of Cherry Tree Farm, and above the now defunct John Turner School to cross Hall Moor Road some two hundred yards south east of the junction of Hall Moor Road and Long Hill. The railway track, still ascending, ran through the Hall Dale wood above Hall Dale Lane to Hall Dale Quarry, which produced a delicate pink coloured stone. The Stancliffe line left the main line near Broad Meadow, at an elevation of about three hundred and twenty feet above sea level. Hall Dale Quarry is around six hundred and thirty feet above sea level. The line ascended some three hundred feet in a journey of about two miles. This was worked in two loops and a dead end, a system often used in mountainous countries. The train first goes downhill to gather momentum, then ascends the loop, reversing its direction of travel at each stop.

Stancliffe standard gauge railway, 1897-1938, had almost three miles of track altogether, powered by two tank engines. One was called "Sir Joseph" and the second, acquired a short time later, was called "Henry Dawson". Another 040 loco called "Canada" helped out when the others were repaired or overhauled. During the First World War women worked in Stancliffe Quarry and yard, and were supplied with boots and corduroy suits by the company. I have heard that some of the rail track was taken up and sent to France at that time, and would be interested to know if anyone can confirm this. Stone continued to be transported by rail from the Hall Dale Quarry until about 1936, when the quarry was closed. About 1939 the track was dismantled. However the rails were still across Hall Moor Road in the 1950s.

I was born and live on Darley Hillside, and as a youngster well remember the sound of the engine exhaust and the clouds of steam as either Sir Joseph or Henry Dawson beat their way up to the Hall Dale with one or two wagons, and also watching the engine going to and fro from the main line to Stancliffe yard. Some of the people residing in Oker Avenue little realise they are living in the very place where the rail tracks ran for forty years. What tales of railway activities this old track bed could tell!.

Mention must here be made of the men who made the railway run – the lengthsmen Adam Travis and Tommy White, drivers Jess Geddes and Matt Cropper and fireman Arthur Fawley, all overseen for many years by John Robert Fearn, grandfather of Councillor David Fearn.

Stancliffe Estates in the 1920s also had a garage, sold petrol, ran a building supplies, had an extensive nursery business, a forestry and woodyard site, and an engineers workshop. Stancliffe also started a precast stone works in the 1920s, and the shops at Broad Walk are built from the Stancliffe Precast Stone.

I believe about two hundred and eighty people were employed by Stancliffe Estates, including up to six blacksmiths. Charles Dawson who was Managing Director of Stancliffe Estates died in 1923 as the result of a car accident near Buxton. His successor as Managing Director was Arthur Morton from Manchester,who also built the South Park (Broad Walk) Estate in the 1930s, having the advantage of the Stancliffe standard gauge track passing by the estate for delivery of building materials. Morton brought the three Ainscough brothers, Harry, Tommy and Bob, with him from Manchester to help build South Park. I had the privilege of working with two of the brothers, and also with a number of the old builders, masons and quarrymen from Stancliffe, who all possessed a wealth of knowledge and skill in all things stone. There are examples of their skills, from pulp stones to buildings containing elaborate masonry, worldwide. Pulp stones for paper making were sold in train loads to Canada, the Americas and Scandinavia.

In 1947 Stancliffe Estates sold up, and a new company was formed to work the quarry called the Stancliffe Stone Company Limited. Another firm still trades and quarries on Stanton Moor under that name but has no connection or access to the original Stancliffe Stone Quarry.

Stancliffe Quarry is still being worked supplying the original Stancliffe Stone to the construction industry nationwide. The waste tips contain over a million tons of stone, ranging from blocks weighing a few hundredweights to those of several tons in weight. It is said that owing to the extensive use of Stancliffe Stone in England, one is never more than twenty miles from a piece of Darley Dale.

MILLCLOSE

The Millclose Mine complex was undoubtedly a great influence on Darley Dale and district for about four hundred years. Millclose was believed to be the old name of the small brook which ran from the Winster area to meet the Derwent just above Darley Bridge.

Milnclose, as it was known in the late 1600s, was first drained by a sough in the 1680s. In 1743 the London Lead Company, who had mined around Winster since the 1720s, took over the Millclose vein working. The mine suffered greatly from flooding, water wheels and a steam engine were both used to drain the mine. The main shaft at this stage was on the north side of the brook which ran from the Winster area west of Cowley Knoll. In 1764 the mine was closed as very little lead was found. This, coupled with the ever present water problems, made the mine unviable.

Between 1764 and 1859, when the Millclose Mine reopened at Watts Shaft, several companies had tried to work the mine and failed. The 1859 venture was led by Edward Wass, who owned the lead smelting works at Lea, near Holloway. Wass erected a huge Cornish steam engine with a 50 inch cylinder developing some 80 h.p. and pumped the mine dry. Workings were extended southwards to under the B5057 Winster Road, but very little lead was found. These workings were abandoned and a level driven northwards, and by the mid 1860s this level had reached the Warren Carr area. Wass had spent £75,000, a fortune in those days, and run out of money. The miners volunteered to continue working the level northwards for nothing and fortunately at this time a rich vein of lead was discovered. By 1874 the mine, though extremely profitable, was being drowned again. All the water was being pumped through Watts shaft which became ever more distant from the working. Millclose closed once again while all efforts were directed to sinking a new shaft at Warren Carr, and making arrangements to install a new giant steam pump which went under the name of Jumbo. This had an 80 inch cylinder, i.e. 2 metres, and 32 millimetres in diameter. It raised 630 gallons, or 2384 litres per minute = 907,200 gallons per day. This new engine and the old one at Watts shaft soon pumped the mine dry and had a fifty per cent spare capacity for future use. By 1878 Millclose had become extremely profitable with the extraction of over three thousand tons of lead ore.

Two more shafts were sunk. No water was raised to the surface. It was pumped into the Yatestoop Sough which ran nearby on its way from Winster to Darley Bridge. In 1889 two more steam pumps were installed, Baby and Alice. E.M. Wass died in 1886 and was buried at St. Helen's Church, Darley Dale.

Millclose miners struck more rich lodes of lead ore over the next fifty years. The smelter was moved from Lea to Millclose around 1934 to cope with increased production. Wass's trustees ran the mine from his death to 1919 when the mine was purchased by the Bradford Vale Mining Company. Millclose Mine Ltd. purchased the mine in 1920 when the Managing Director was George Henry Key.

In 1922 Consolidated Goldfields purchased a major share in the mine and invested large sums of money in it. Huge amounts of lead were found under the area from Stanton Lees towards Rowsley. 1936 saw a resurgence of the old enemy, water. The mine by now had reached a depth of approximately 1,000 feet (over 213 metres). On 25th February 1938 Fred Boam of Winster blasted a hole into the Pilhough Fault. Water poured in and flooded the mine and four hundred miners were temporarily laid off. It took ten weeks and extra pumps to pump out the water. Approximately eight million gallons a day in total were flooding into the mine and despite all efforts the mine finally ceased working in June 1940. The smelter was purchased by H.J .Enthoven & Sons in 1941 and is still in production refining scrap lead.

Eight hundred men were employed at the mine and smelter in the mid 1930s. It was the largest and most productive lead mine in Europe. Four hundred and thirty thousand tons of galena (lead ore) were raised between 1861 and 1939, yielding approximately three hundred and fifty thousand tons of lead, worth over £100m at today's prices. With the death of the four hundred years old Millclose Mine lead mining came to an end in our valley.

The author's brother John William Jackson of Darley Hillside, and Patrick Devaney of Green Lane, Darley Dale, worked on the pumps at the time of the great flood. Watts Shaft and engine house are well worth a visit. They are located west of the old road to Birchover at the rear of H.J. Enthoven's smelter, where the trackway/footpath splits off for Winster and Wensley Top.

THE NURSERIES

JAMES SMITH & SONS'

DARLEY DALE NURSERIES

The Founder of the Firm.

Near MATLOCK, DERBYSHIRE.

The Late Proprietor.

The Present Proprietor.

Darley Dale has a long history of nurseries with its acid based soils and its range of elevations, from the valley floor at 312 feet (95 metres), to the high moors at 1,000 feet (305 metres).

Nurserying took place on the eastern slopes, which received the most sun, was protected from the harsh cold winds, and was adequately served with water from the springs which ran from under the gritstone cap. The Hall Dale was well watered and screened from the worst of the weather and the soil was very fertile. Plants were started around the 394 feet (120m.) contour, then moved to suitable locations at much higher levels. This made the plants very hardy.

Heathers, rhododendrons, evergreen plants all thrived. Areas of the nurseries were dedicated to growing trees three to seven metres high specifically for transplanting. It took three years to prepare a semi-mature tree for transplanting. These trees were sent all over Britain and Europe, roots wrapped in sacking, and each protected by a wicker cage made from pollarded willow branches. There was a willow plantation at the rear of St. Helen's Church and another at Siberia Nursery, now the Darwin Forest Holiday Park. Almost two hundred men and boys were employed by the various nurseries, the most famous being James Smith & Sons (Darley Dale) Nurseries. Founded in the 1770s the business became established in Darley Dale in 1827. The nurseries were about two hundred and fifty acres (approximately one hundred hectares) in extent.

About one thousand tons of trees and shrubs were dispatched from Darley Dale Station every year. Customers included Royal Estates in Britain and Europe, the Botanic Gardens at Kew, Edinburgh, Dublin and many other city parks, municipal gardens and streets. In the early 1900s, when the nursery was at its peak, its stock included 300,000 rhododendrons, upwards of a million coniferous trees, shrubs, fruit trees, 30,000 rose trees, hundreds of thousands of heather plants, and innumerable stocks of other plants, from tree ivies in pots to lilacs.

The principal nursery areas in Darley Dale were Home, Siberia North, Canada, Butchers Lane, Station, Churchtown, Hall Moor, Bent, Hill Top, Wheatley Roundhills, Willsitch, and Hall Dale.

These Nurseries are very exposed, ranging from 400 feet up to 1,100 feet above sea level.

By Appointment:

NURSERY CATALOGUE, 1931-32.

JAMES SMITH & SONS,

DARLEY DALE NURSERIES,
Near MATLOCK.

TELEGRAMS : "SMITHIANA TWO DALES,"   TELEPHONE No. 7, DARLEY DALE.

Transplanted Forest Trees.

	Height	Doz. s. d.	100 s. d.	1000 s. d.
ALDER (*Alnus*)				
common	1 to 1¼ft.	—	4 0	30 0
,,	1½ to 2 ft.	—	5 0	40 0
,,	6 to 7 ft.	5 0	—	—
white	5 to 6 ft.	4 0	—	—
,,	6 to 7 ft.	6 0	—	—
ASH (*Fraxinus*)				
common	1 to 1¼ft.	—	5 0	40 0
,,	1¼ to 2 ft.	—	8 0	60 0
,,	2 to 3 ft.	—	10 0	80 0
mountain (Rowan Tree)	1 to 1¼ft.	—	5 0	40 0
,, ,,	2 to 3 ft.	—	12 0	—
,, ,,	5 to 6 ft.	6 0	40 0	—
,, ,,	6 to 7 ft.	8 0	50 0	—

No connection with any other firm. Please note all our Stationery bears the Royal Coat of Arms, **by Appointment.**
To avoid letters reaching other hands, it is very important all communications should be addressed in full to:—
JAMES SMITH & SONS,
DARLEY DALE NURSERIES,
Near MATLOCK.

	Height	Doz. s. d.	100 s. d.	1000 s. d.
BEECH (*Fagus*)				
common	1 to 1¼ft.	—	6 0	50 0
,,	1¼ to 2 ft.	—	8 0	70 0
,,	2 to 3 ft.	—	15 0	120 0
,,	3 to 3½ft.	4 0	25 0	—
BIRCH (*Betula*)				
common	5 to 6 ft.	3 0	20 0	—
,,	7 to 8 ft.	12 0	—	—
white (silver)	15 to 20 in.	—	6 0	50 0
,, ,,	2 to 3 ft.	—	12 0	—
,, ,,	6 to 7 ft.	12 0	—	—
,, ,,	7 to 8 ft.	15 0	—	—

1

Home Staff of James Smith and Sons' Darley Dale Nurseries

Consignment about to leave the nurseries for HIM the Emperor of Germany. Potsdam

Choice named Rhododendrons in Wheatley Nursery

A brake of white heather (Erica Vagans Alba Multiflora) Siberia Nursery

The popular heather Erica Darleyensis was discovered as a hybrid growing in James Smith's nurseries. James Smith Darley Dale Nurseries are now defunct.

Henry Derbyshire of Darley Hillside commenced nurserying around 1870 and moved to Springfield on Foggs Hill at the time of the First World War. The Derbyshires also specialised in heathers and rhododendrons and the family still live at Springfield. Their once extensive nursery is now much reduced.

Hugh Gregory & Son nursery occupied the area on Darley Hillside between Moor Lane, Hall Moor Road, and Gill Lane. The Gregory family live in the eighteenth century Orchard Cottage on the site of their nursery. Their business, like the Derbyshires' is much reduced from earlier times.

Stancliffe Estates also had an extensive nursery from 1898 until 1947, with its headquarters at Fircliffe on Fircliffe Lane, off Whitworth Road. The company nurseried the area adjacent to Bent Lane, south of Bumper Castle Farm, above the Darley Dale Waterworks at White Springs Farm, Sir Joseph Whitworth's private garden area now called Highlands, and land between Whitworth Road and Stancliffe Quarry, now Sir Joseph's Lane.

Highlands Conservatory, used by Stancliffe Nursery, was demolished in the late 1920s and the walled garden/nursery area let. The manager of Stancliffe Nurseries from their inception until the 1920s was Walter Wall, former head gardener to Sir Joseph and Lady Whitworth. He lived in the lodge to Stancliffe Gardens, Whitworth Road, now known as Highlands. The barn to Fircliffe House situated on the old road from the top of Church Lane to Northwood was used as a packing shed. Joseph Allsop spent his working life at Stancliffe Nurseries.

James Charlesworth & Son, upper Hackney, Darley Dale, was founded by James Charlesworth in the late 1800s. He began operations at the Bleachcroft, Ladygrove, Two Dales, east of the Mill, and later acquired land at Hackney. These five acres of south west facing slopes became the firm's main nursery. The third generation of Charlesworths continue to run it. Almost all their stock is propagated at the nursery, which, similarly to other Darley nurseries, specialises in hardy trees and shrubs, rhododendrons, conifers and hedging plants which are. supplied to garden centres, landscape firms and retail outlets over a wide area.

TRANSPORT FIRMS

Two hundred and fifty years ago the roads through our valley were little more than tracks and great changes in modes of transport have taken place in the valley since then. After the Enclosure Acts of the 1700s the beginnings of the turnpike toll roads helped to meet the demands of the Industrial Revolution, which began early in the area with the local lead, stone and cotton industries.

The opening of the Cromford canal in 1794, followed by the railway in 1849, ensured good communication with the rest of Britain. This growth of industry so overloaded the main road through the valley that in 1830/32 it was upgraded and re-routed. A new toll house was built at the junction of Old Road and Dale Road (A6) near the bottom of Greenaway Lane, and the Grouse Inn was built at Darleys in the Dale. The A6 has been continuously improved ever since, culminating in the widening of Cromford Tors in 1965.

After the railways arrived in 1849 the stage coach and canal businesses declined and the viability of the canal ceased in 1903. Local coaches and charabancs battled on until the end of the First World War, mostly running between towns which had no direct rail link, including Ashbourne, Matlock and Chesterfield. Within another fifty years the railway through the valley had gone. One hundred and twenty years of rail transport vanished like the one hundred and twenty years of stage coaching and the one hundred and ten or so years of canal transport into the valley, all superceded by the internal combustion engine.

As internal combustion engines became more reliable they signalled the demise of horse drawn transport, and the era following the end of the First World War saw the beginning of taxis, buses and lorries. Our valley was ideally situated for long distance transport, being in the centre of England, astride the main London to Carlisle road

After the First World War motor taxis appeared. Dick Lane from Darley Hillside, Fred Wilson from Park Lane, Two Dales, Jim Woolliscroft and Mr. Slack who both lived on Stancliffe View, near Green Lane all ran taxis. Bus services were run by Slacks, Woolliscrofts, Hands and North Western. Charabancs were owner driven, like Fred Wilson with his charabanc "Bluebell". There were all makes of vehicles, from Thorneycrofts to Model T Fords. Lorry fleets were run by families whose names are still familiar today – Furniss, Waters, Lowe, Toft and Tomlinson, George Siddall and Toplis, driven by men whose sons and grandsons still roam Britain and even further afield today, at the wheel of immense sophisticated vehicles.

We must not forget the steam traction engine drivers who drove for Caudwells, Gregory's wood mills, local quarries and local agricultural contractors. At the end of the 1926 General Strike the late Jim Toplis of Darley Dale drove a steam traction engine with three trailers to Immingham for a load of sugar from the docks. The total journey took ten days, and the strike was over before he returned. More about the Toplis brothers later.

In the 1890s a young girl called Daisy Watson worked for Lady Whitworth at Stancliffe Hall. She met and married James Henry Woolliscroft, who ran a horse drawn van round Darley selling fruit and vegetables. Around the time of the First World War he acquired a Model T ford for his business, which also doubled as a taxi and soon became a charabanc. The Green Lane housing triangle, Darley Dale, was built prior to the first world war, and James Henry and Daisy moved into the second of the two shops at Stancliffe View, opposite the bottom of Whitworth Road. James Henry kept his vehicles in Stancliffe Works yard. He painted his buses silver and called his company the "Silver Service". Business boomed. Bus services were provided to local villages, with trips to the seaside and the Sunday mystery trips to visit the lovely peakland villages and scenery of our county. These trips were at their most popular during the 1930s, enabling young and old alike to visit places they otherwise would never have seen.

In 1928/29 a new garage was built next to Darley House, at the

248

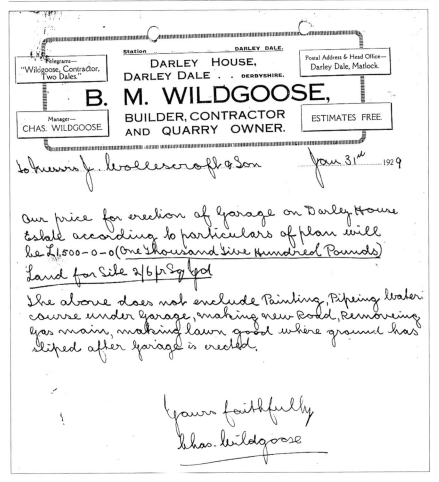

Price for Wooliscroft's new garage at the bottom of Hackney Lane January 1929

bottom of Hackney Lane, now occupied by Milner Conversions. James Henry's son James Watson Woolliscroft took over the business in the 1950s, followed by his three sons Selwyn, John and Peter in 1971. They reached a peak of about thirty buses after taking over Hulleys of Baslow in 1977. In 1989 Hulleys was sold off in a management buy-out, and Woolliscrofts ceased trading in 1990.

Woolliscroft horse and cart

Still wearing his leggings with first motor van

Did the van become this charabanc?

The first bus

1938 bus known as the dummy front

Woolliscroft bus in Stancliffe yard 1920s with number 5

Matlock to Darley Dale return ticket 6d 2^1/2p

Left to right: Martin Waters (son), Nick Waters (son), Tim Waters (son),
Roger Jepson (nephew of Nick), Dominic Waters (son of Tim), Jack Cundill (driver),
Tommy Kirk (driver), Donald Spigg (driver)

Bernard John Waters, Station Road, Darley Dale 1928

Knight Brothers started at Stanton 1920s, Wally F Marsden 1947, finished trading 2001

Woolliscrofts, in common with other bus services, employed female conductors from the beginning of the Second World War. Among these were Ethel and Lucy Wain., Kathleen Stephenson and Kath Fielding. Drivers included George and Wilfred Woodhouse, who between them had over sixty years service. Stan Blaydon and Connie Smith worked in the office for forty-eight years. The 1940s wartime buses had unusual seating arrangements. All the seats were placed longways on around the sides, so that more standing passengers could be accommodated in the middle. The last buses left Matlock at 9 p.m.

William Henry Furniss drove the horse drawn fire engine serving the Darley Dale area, which was kept in a building now demolished which stood in the Derbyshire Dales District Council's car park at the rear of the present Town Hall. The horses, which were kept in adjacent fields, were very loathe to be caught and harnessed to the fire engine, as they knew a very strenuous time was ahead as William Henry, dressed in a bright red coat, galloped them helter skelter to the fire; this could lead to delays. William Henry served in the First World War and lost a leg.

Waters Transport, a four-generation lorry firm, commenced business with a Thorneycroft or AEC lorry in Stancliffe yard in 1923. They were nationalised in 1949 and after de-nationalisation in 1954 they recommenced business at Darley Bridge in a garage shared with another local haulier George Siddall, who was taken over by Waters in 1974. Amongst Waters drivers were Jack Large, Les Holmes and Jack Cundy. Waters ran Commer trucks after the war, and they now have a fleet of fifty heavy goods vehicles based at two depots, and run into Europe.

George Siddall, first based at Stanton in the Peak, started in the early 1930s with mostly tipping lorries, carting stone and carrying out contract work for local Councils. In 1947 the company moved to Darley Bridge, where in 1948/9, working as a young builder for David Sheldon (an associate firm of Hall & Co., Matlock), I worked on the new garage. George Siddall, at his peak, had about twenty vehicles.

Frank Toplis Transport worked from the garage, now a shop and petrol station on the A6 at Darley Dale opposite the entrance to D.F.S. Frank started the firm with one lorry, a Chevrolet, in the early 1920s, carting lead ore from Mill Close Mine to the smelter at Lea. While on the subject of lead ore carting, in or about 1929 a Garrat six-wheel steam wagon, so loaded with ore and heavy at the rear that its steering was affected, failed to negotiate Darley Bridge and went through the parapet and toppled into the river.

Toplis's and other firms expanded in the 1930s as our valley became even more prosperous. Toplis's drivers included Bill Grindy, Harry Bispham, Fred Walker, Jack Cowley and Ernie Walker (now the owner of Walker's Transport, Cromford). Toplis, like Toft and Tomlinson, also ran long distance tramping lorries. Frank died in 1945. His brother Jim, of the steam traction engine expedition to Immingham, and Frank's son Harold ran the firm until nationalisation in 1949. In 1947 Toplis's made and ran an articulated lorry. The tractor unit was adapted from a Bedford army lorry. At its peak Toplis's had about 14 heavy goods vehicles. Jim died in 1990 and Harold in 2000. A typical wage for a lorry driver in the 1930s was under £2 per week.

Richard Henry Lowe, whose home town was Manchester, started in business in 1920 with a Ford Model T lorry. In 1938 he was appointed Transport Manager with Toft and Tomlinson, and settled in Northwood Lane. Mr.Lowe went into business on his own account in 1945 as Lowe's Transport with a few ex-army lorries, Bedfords and Internationals, fitted with Perkins diesel engines. Lorries fitted with Perkins diesels usually had a symbol composed of rings fitted on the vehicle front, a familiar sight in the post war years, as many ex-army petrol lorries were converted to diesel. Lowe's, under its later name of Lowe Brothers Transport became the Matlock Transport company, and for a few years had a mixed fleet of tippers and flats. Eric and Alf Lowe, two of Richard Lowe's four sons, have now retired after one hundred years between them in the business. Lowes (Matlock Transport) now run about fifty heavy goods vehicles. Grandchildren .now work in the firm – another three generation company. A word about nationalisation. The Labour government's Nationalisation Act of 1949 which created British Road Services, took in all transport firms who travelled more than twenty-five miles (over 40 kilometres) away from their operating base. Frank Toplis and Toft and Tomlinson were the principal firms taken over. BRS was de-nationalised in 1954.

James Albert Toft, 1866 to 1936, was a blacksmith at Youlgreave. Born to a world of horses he lived to see his two sons and son-in-law with the largest fleet of lorries in the district, about seventy or eighty. Eli and Vernon Toft, and brother-in-law Jim Tomlinson, commenced business in 1922 at Youlgreave, on the site where the village surgery now stands. They ran two steam lorries, a Clayton Shuttleworth and a Sentinel, soon acquiring some motor lorries. In 1928 they moved to North Darley, on sites on each side of the A6 at Deeley Town. Their cousin Ezra Toft, a builder, also from Youlgrave, built them a terrace of three houses, and across the road a large new garage. The houses were named Unity Villas, and the vehicle premises Unity Garage. The roof for the original garage was from a First World War aeroplane hangar. These premises are still known as the Unity Complex, and are still associated with transport, housing four transport-connected firms – Tollbar Racing,

Darley Dale Garage, Two Dales Body Repair and Paint workshop, and T.D.I. Tipsafe vehicle support systems.

Tofts pioneered the use of diesel engines in HGVs and around 1930 became the main agents for Gardner diesel engines for the East Midlands. Jim Tomlinson's sons Albert and Bill took over the reins of the firm in the early 1940s. After the war the firm ran about ninety lorries, and had another company called North Derbyshire Engineering, contracting out civil engineering plant. Toft's lorries roamed the length and breadth of Britain, driven by men who knew the best way to anywhere, working very long hours in draughty, noisy machines. The engine was literally in the cab with the driver, red hot in summer and freezing in winter. There were no heaters or syncromesh gear boxes, brakes which were not the best, and no power steering. These lorries had to be driven with great skill, always planning two hundred and fifty yards ahead. There were no fork lift trucks, Hiab cranes and pallets then. Most days the driver had ten or twelve tons of goods to be loaded and unloaded by hand and then a night's lodging to find.

Ron Wragg was the fleet engineer in the post- war years, including the time of nationalisation. Following the break-up of B.R.S. the firms were run by the Tomlinson and McLean families as Toft Brothers and Tomlinson (1954) Limited. They also purchased and ran Dalton Quarries at Stoney Middleton. The 1950s saw HGV gross weights increasing, resulting in suspension problems, i.e. broken springs. My cousin Len Jackson, who was in charge of servicing at the time, thought there must be another type of suspension besides steel springs. He found an alternative on the London tube trains of the day, a rubber/metal sandwich. After much discussion with Ron Wragg and the directors it was decided to produce a new type of suspension, and a new heavy goods vehicle to go with it.

HGVs at this time were limited to twenty-four tons gross. The new Toft HGV was designed for twenty-eight tons gross, and to be an articulated vehicle, ie one with a propulsion unit – the tractor – separate from the body. The men who built it from scratch were Len Jackson, Gilbert Davis, Bill Needham, Sam Foxlow and driver Frank Blair. Ron

Wragg pooled all the ideas and then converted them into plans to work from. The lorry was called the NORDE, after the North Derbyshire Engineering Company, as was the unique rubber/metal suspension they built for it. Powered by a Cummins NTO-6-B 12-litre 6-cylinder turbo charged diesel engine the NORDE, after very few teething problems, was an outstanding success. The M1 and other motorways were in their infancy, as was the NORDE, and they made a perfect combination. Capable of seventy miles per hour the NORDE cruised the M1 fully laden, never dropping below sixty miles per hour, passing many cars. Frank Blair, its driver, became renowned, as did his brother Laurence who drove it when Frank was not available. When empty it would out-accelerate quite a few cars of that era. Tofts expected many orders for the NORDE but non materialised. However another NORDE, a six-wheeler rigid, was built. The NORDE Suspension System went on to be a success, and is still being built today by Hendrickson. Four NORDES were built altogether; one was operated by Longcliffe Quarries and all had a long and successful operating life. The articulated NORDE was eventually purchased by Roger Geeson, vehicle dismantlers at Pentrich, for scrap. So died a legend, and so virtually died the British lorry industry, to be replaced by innovative Volvo, Scania, Mercedes, and Isuzu who are now the world's largest truck makers.

In the 1970s the Toft companies went into receivership, and the firm was wound up. Over fifty years experience in the golden age of transport ceased. Tofts had many long time employees – Albert Prince, who started at Youlgreave and served the company for forty-eight years on the maintenance side, joiner Joe Derbyshire, body and cab builder, Fred Billinge, painter/signwriter and long distance drivers Eric Ainscough, Albert Geeson, Tom Talbot, Jack Mills, the Blair brothers, and Alf Moody who sadly died when his lorry crashed into the Derwent opposite the Boathouse Inn at Matlock. Many truly excellent men passed through Toft Brothers & Tomlinson, on their way up in the transport world, including managers, mechanics, transport operators and drivers – a great team with unbounded loyalty on both sides and expertise in the transport field for over fifty years.

Ron Wragg as fleet engineer was outstanding; to design and build a HGV which was years ahead of its time, based only on practical experience in the workshop and on the road, was remarkable. Ron's first wife was also in transport, driving her own taxi for many years, based at Northwood Lane. It would be almost impossible to build the 1961 NORDE today without the backing of a multi-national HGV manufacturer, with a main frame computer, because of the weight of rules and regulations, and the administration required to pass the vehicle fit for road use. The transport industry today, like most other industries, carries an immense burden of legislation, enforced by an army of administrators. Transport has headed the bankruptcy list for many years. To survive three or four generations in it is noteworthy.

Around 1910 the Fox family moved to this area to work at Caudwell's Mill, Rowsley. One son George, born in 1896, served in the first world war, and 1922 saw him driving a solid tyred bus on the demanding Clowne via Chesterfield to Matlock Bath run. Around 1927/28 George was bus driving for William Furniss, followed by a spell in 1928/33 with North Western. In 1933 George decided to go lorry driving for Toft Brothers & Tomlinson. He moved to Shands in 1941, driving machinery and materials to the new wartime shadow factory being constructed on the L.M.S. sports ground at Deeley Town (now Firth Rixsons). George drove a 1930s chain-driven Scammel, a leviathan among vehicles. A journey to Scotland and back with a large excavator took about a week (twenty miles per hour top speed!). George's son Joseph followed in his father's footsteps, starting at Tofts, then Derbyshire Stone, followed by thirty-seven years at Shands, latterly as transport manager. The Fox family were typical HGV and PSV men, who lived and worked through the primary years of internal combustion engined transport, from the one-ton to the thirty-eight ton HGV, and fourteen-seater charabanc to the fifty-seater motorway express bus, from virtually no rules to an absolute plethora of regulations covering everything from the size and number of wheelnuts to physical fitness and compulsory tea breaks.

Two Dales taxi

Caudwells steam lorry at Derby

Caudwell Mill April 1921

George Siddal Transport at Stanton in the Peak

George Siddall, Darley Bridge

Gregory's of Darley Dale taken in Dale Road, Matlock

Gregory's outside Twiggs A6 Dale Road, Matlock

Tofts Transport make the headlines with the Norde

263

George Fox with bus from Clowne to Matlock Bath at the Pavilion

The Fox family 1930s

The period after the Second World War, 1946 to 1956, owing to the scarcity of new HGVs, saw many ex-army vehicles and ex-army drivers appear on the roads. Lowes at Darley Dale converted several army Bedfords to diesel. Gregory's at Victoria Saw Mills ran huge Matadors made by AEC, converted into winch and crane vehicles by employee Vic Carter. Most medium to heavy army lorries had four and six-wheel drive, some with unusual wheel arrangements. Harry Evans acquired a small fleet of American ex-army six-wheel drive lorries and adapted them for lime spreading. Driving them on Derbyshire's rugged hills was a daily adventure. One of his drivers, Bert Smith from Cromford, launched himself with a six-wheel drive GMC ex-American Army truck, fully laden with lime one wet morning down the front of Masson. Three fields and two walls later he managed to stop it before, as he remarked at the time "the going got rough". Longcliffe Quarries also ran a few American ex-army GMC lorries. All these lorries were left hand drive, with huge long bonnets stuck out in front, and semi cabs with canvas roofs, very rakish looking vehicles.

The RASC had a driver training school at the Whitworth Institute from 1940 to 1946. Learner drivers used to travel in convoys of about twenty vehicles, shepherded by men on motor cycles. When they were practising three-point turns, no walls or pedestrians were safe. Darley folk became very alert at the appearance of these learner convoys. Several of the soldiers married local girls and stayed in the area. Two who spring to mind are Jim Boyack and Stan Blaydon. Stan drove a Silver Service bus for forty years. I remember one afternoon in late 1943 when a huge convoy of tanks on, I believe, Thorneycroft tank transporters, came to Darley. They unloaded the tanks and dispersed them under the trees around Stancliffe Hall park, where they stayed for a couple of days. Two light tanks with rubber pads parked in the Grouse Inn yard. Some time in the war a convoy of Quads (smallish army towing lorries), towing guns, went down the notorious Sydnope Hill at Two Dales. Disaster struck, as the brakes failed on one of the rear Quads causing a multiple shunt, resulting in a shambles of crashed vehicles and guns, and dead, dying and injured soldiers littered the hillside.

Local lorry drivers are very aware of the dangers of our steep hills, but drivers from reasonably flat areas soon find out the braking capabilities of their laden lorries when negotiating such steep winding roads as Cromford Hill, Sydnope Hill and Chesterfield Road at Matlock. All these roads have seen many horrendous crashes this century, including steam waggons. The Second World War, with its total absence of signposts, headlights almost completely blacked out, bombing raids on towns and cities, was to say the least a very testing time for HGV drivers, who were mostly very young or well into middle age; all the rest had been called up for active service.

Here are just a few of the haulage firms from around the district whose vehicles were, and in some cases still are, familiar sights on our valley's roads, owned or run by men with "wheels in the blood". Alfie Smith (followed by Denzil Smith), Dakin Brothers and Wally Smith, all of Matlock; Sid Cook of Wessington; Shimwells of Youlgrave; Loxleys of Bonsall; Knight Brothers and Shirley Proctor of Rowsley; Phillips of Wirksworth, and Gregorys of Slinter Lane, Cromford, Toft and Tomlinson, Darley Dale. Other companies operating their own HGVs included the Long Rake Spar Company, Middleton by Youlgrave, The Express Dairy Co., Rowsley, S. & E. Johnson, Corn Merchants of Two Dales, Hoveringham's Dene Quarry, Cromford, Derbyshire Stone Limited, B.J. Waters Ltd, George Sidall and Lowes Transport (now Matlock Transport). This is by no means a comprehensive list.

From early this century to the 1950s the bicycle was the everyday means of transport for millions of people for work and leisure. Policemen, postmen, delivery boys, railway men and shift workers all depended on two wheels to carry out their work. Almost every village had a cycle sale and repair shop – Darley Dale's was at the top of Station Road. The bicycle has never been surpassed as a cheap reliable means of transport, from the penny-farthing to the latest vogue, the mountain bike.

Transport of all types has been a major factor in the evolution of our valley from pack horses, stage coaches, canals and railways to cars, buses and HGV. The twentieth century's meteoric advance in road transport not only shaped our valley, it has changed the world. There are still one or two people alive in our valley today who have lived through this momentous period. Darley Dale is one of the few places in Britain where it is still commonplace to see an 1800s stage coach followed by the latest juggernaught HGV with computer controlled systems. The old vehicle is from the Red House Carriage Museum, near the site of the old toll house at the junction of the A6 and Old Road, which has a fleet of horse-drawn carriages and coaches. If the nineteenth century was the birth of the Industrial Revolution, the twentieth century has most certainly been the birth of internal combustion engine powered road transport.

JOHNSON'S MILL

Johnsons Millers commenced business in 1861 at Eagle Torr, Birchover, and the remains of the wall of the dam which powered the water wheel are still in situ. There is no trace of the mill itself.

J .W. Johnson, Millers, had moved to Middleton-by-Youlgrave by the late 1860s, living in the village and milling in Middleton Dale until around 1896, after which they rented Alport Mill from the Duke of Rutland. Each move was for an improvement in the supply of water to drive the machinery.

In 1924 Ladygrove Flax Mill, owned by the Dakeyne Estate, came up for sale along with the rest of their estate. Johnsons purchased the mill and the three dams complex which supplied the mill with an ample water supply. The machinery was driven by a turbine supplied by Gilbert Gilkes from Kendal in 1894. The turbine worked until 1963 when an accident ruined it. It was rebuilt with more modern bearings and ran until 1979. The turbine and its water supply are still in position. Before the turbine was installed the mill was powered by a sixty feet head of water working three water wheels at once in vertical formation. There is believed to be only one other site in Europe which used three water wheels in vertical unison. The period from 1925 to 1938 saw a large increase in business.

In 1937 Johnsons Mill, which was now run by the two brothers Ernest and Sydney Johnson, purchased the Old Road factory. This factory was formerly the home of the Bakelite Company from the early to the late 1920s and at the time of purchase was owned by Mr. Ward of Wards brewery, Sheffield , who had lived for a time at Aston Lane, Oker, in a large house built by Twyfords around the 1920s. This house did not survive and no trace of it remains. S. & E. Johnson had only been in the Old Road Mill two and a half years when it was requisitioned by the government as a Shadow Factory for Bakelite, the former occupants. Upon de-requisitioning in 1946 Johnsons moved back to Old Road. Charles Maddox and his wife moved back into the manager's house which he had first occupied in 1939 when he married. Charles and Margaret lived there for nearly forty years. Porridge oats, puffed wheat

Johnson's Ladygrove Mill
Bell Tower site of the three waterwheels and water pipe feed for the turbine
Rear view of mill

and cornflakes were produced at the Ladygrove Mill during and just after the second war. Local women, including Mrs Marjorie Gregory, helped to keep the mill running while the men were away at war.

Walton Corn Mill, now part of the DFS site, was used by Johnsons after the war for the production of mineral mixes, then converted in 1960 to produce biscuit flour. Production ceased at the Walton Mill site about 1970 and for a short time the site became a Night Club and Restaurant called The Maple Leaf.

At the height of the business after the war Johnsons Millers employed over one hundred and forty people. They ran a large transport fleet, from horse and drays, then a steam lorry, a Buick lorry before the second war, to a fleet of heavy goods vehicles, including modern 38-ton articulated lorries. In the late 1940s and 50s power cuts were commonplace. Johnsons Ladygrove Mill generated their own electricity to take over and supplement the national grid supply. Johnsons left the Old Road site in 2001, concentrating production at Ladygrove. Johnsons and their employees had a special bond. Harry Slaney worked at the mills for fifty years and many other men spent most of their life working there, including Richard and Charles Maddox, Fred Waller, George Roberts, Fred Batterley, Derek Witcher, George and Harold Wardman, Gilbert Bacon, Michael Gibbs, Peter Buchan, Cyril Thraves, Frank Hodgkinson, Fred Harrison, Maurice Ollerenshaw, Cliff Marsden, Charles Armishaw, Graham Land, Ken Knowles, Bill Baker, Peter Riley and many others. More than fifty watches have been presented to employees with twenty-five years and more service. Ernest Johnson's daughter Christine, who was highly involved with the business, still lives in the area, and Mr. David Westmoreland, Sydney Johnson's stepson, is now the Chairman after spending forty-three years working at the Mills.

In 1789 Daniel Dakeyne acquired the newly erected textile mill situated on the Ladygrove Brook at Two Dales. He commenced business there but the business did not prosper and thirteen years later in 1802 the firm of Daniel Dakeyne and Sons went bankrupt. The Mill was advertised for sale, also Knabb House, The Holt, thirty acres of land, and a 'Childrens Lodge' capable of housing up to one hundred children. No worthwhile offer was received and two years later, in 1804, the Mill was again put up for sale by auction. What next happened to the Mill property is not known, but by 1839 the Mill property was in the ownership of Daniel's brothers Edward and James.

In 1794 Edward and James, despite their youth (22 and 24), invented a machine for the processing of flax prior to being spun which they named the Equalinium. The Equalinium is often confused with the Disc engine which Edward and James patented in 1830. "A hydraulic machine for communicatory motion to machinery" was the description given to the patented disc engine. It was a marvellous example of ingenuity. Like a jet engine it had only one main moving part. This moving part, the disc, which was the source of the rotary motion, did not itself rotate, an apparent contradiction of its action. The disc had a perfect sphere approximately half its diameter fixed in the centre of the disc. The disc, with its sphere, was fixed in an iron chamber, the sphere resting on a matching concave cone. Another matching concave cone was fixed over the sphere. The upper cone had an opening in its centre some three feet across, and an arm was fixed to the top of the sphere at right angles to the disc. The disc had a slot in it which fitted around a plate in the chamber which ran from the chamber side to, but not touching, the sphere. By admitting water under pressure on one side of the plate, and letting it exhaust on the other side, the disc, which could not rotate, was made to tilt progressively. The progressive tilt of the disc, which was maintained at an approximate angle of 20 degrees to the horizontal, applied a rotary motion to the arm of the sphere.

If you are now as confused as I was when I read the description of the machine, place a dinner plate on a tennis ball and progressively tilt the plate without rotating it and all will become clear.

It is my belief that water, under the same pressure as that which fed the engine,was fed to the underside of the sphere, thereby supporting the disc and making it friction free, also helping to maintain a seal at the gasket on a collar between the opening on the top cone and the sphere.

It is known that this type of engine was later adapted to be run by steam and at least one Royal Navy ship, HMS Minx, was powered by a

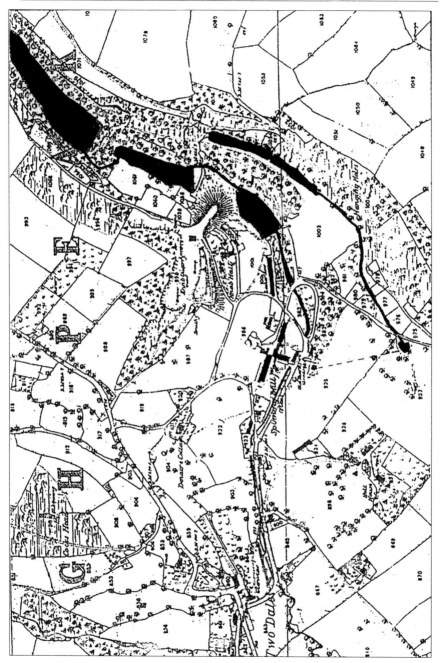

Part of the 1880 edition of the 1/2500 Ordnance Survey map showing the positions of the dams, the leat and the header pond for the engine feed pipeline at Dakeyne's Flax Mill, Ladygrove

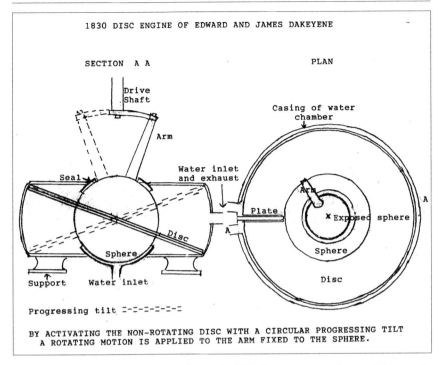

1830 DISC ENGINE OF EDWARD AND JAMES DAKEYENE

SECTION A A

PLAN

Drive Shaft

Casing of water chamber

Arm

Water inlet and exhaust

Seal

Plate

Exposed sphere

A

Disc

Sphere

Sphere

Support   Water inlet

Disc

Progressing tilt

BY ACTIVATING THE NON-ROTATING DISC WITH A CIRCULAR PROGRESSING TILT A ROTATING MOTION IS APPLIED TO THE ARM FIXED TO THE SPHERE.

steam version of the disc engine. HMS Minx was a substantial vessel, approximately three hundred feet long.

By the 1890s disc engines were only a memory, superceded by the turbine which was twice as efficient and still had only the one moving part. A turbine, unlike the disc engine, realised the full potential of the water/steam pressure.

The disc engine is reputed by Phil Wigfull to have replaced the overshot water wheels which drove the Mill at that time, 1804 to 1833. When the brothers built their new Mill in 1826 that was probably the time when the two normal overshot wheels were replaced by the three vertical ones, one above the other working in unison.

The disc engine was fed from a leat from the top dam (Potter) on the Hackney side of the valley to a small header dam about 96 feet above the engine, then by a pipeline to the engine which was situated across the road from the Mill. The remains of the stone retaining walls can still

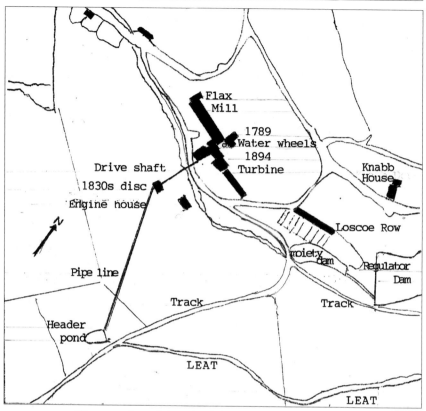

Water supply to disc engine based on a tithe map of 1839

be seen there. A water turbine of 60 h.p. was installed at the Mill below the Bell Tower in 1894, manufactured by Gilbert Gilkes, which ran smoothly and efficiently until an accident befell it in 1963.

The turbine was rebuilt and ran again until 1979, and is still in position complete with its water supply. Ladygrove Mill has been used for many purposes, starting as a Cotton Mill in 1789, extended in 1826 with other considerable extensions, and a serious fire in the 1900s. Two hundred and twenty-two years after the Mill was first constructed it is still going strong.

The first Cotton Mill in the County was erected at Cromford in 1771 by Richard Arkwright, also powered by water.

THE DARLEY CO-OPS

In 1942, when the Second World War was not going well for Britain and its Empire, the author lived opposite Darley Dale's Co-op, now Costcutters, at Crowstones Road. Mr. A. Shimwell from Youlgrave was the manager, Miss M. Wall managed the Ladies department, and I became employed there as errand boy, sweeper-up, cleaner, packager of various goods, boiler stoker and counter hand when I was just fifteen.

In the first year I discovered the miracles of how to bone a side of bacon and name all the different parts, break open the barrels containing two half-hundredweight cheeses made in various Commonwealth countries, and cut it up with cheese wire, and weigh rice, sugar and flour in bags of various weights for stock, all on brass balance scales which had to be cleaned and polished daily. Oranges and bananas were not imported from 1939 to 1946. Most goods came loose, from yeast in seven pound bags to sugar in two-hundredweight sacks, all types of dried fruits in boxes and sacks, flour in ten-stone sacks, animal and poultry feed in one-hundredweight sacks. Coffee beans came in fifty-six pound sacks to be ground by hand and packed in quarter pounds. Bacon came in "sides", ie half a pig, potatoes in one-hundredweight bags, usually very dirty. Sacks of soap flakes were a nightmare – if we were short of bags it was a work of art to parcel them up in a sheet of wrapping paper. The packing had to be perfect so that the soap flakes did not contaminate the rest of the groceries. I can still, in an instant, make a bag out of a plain sheet of paper which will hold water. Twist tobacco came in a roll, shag tobacco in tins, all to be weighed out in ounces, cigarettes in packets, from five Woodbines to ten Park Drive, Capstan, Players, Craven A, and Silkcut in twenty packs.

When you had learned to pack all grocery items you were turned loose on the provisions counter. Butter, lard and margarine mostly came in half-hundredweight boxes, usually made of wood, lined with grease-proof paper. We had wooden butter pats which were kept in a clean jar of water. The fats were cut and shaped into half and quarter pounds. If I remember correctly the weekly food ration of 1942/43 was 8 oz. sugar, 2 oz butter, 2 oz lard, 4 oz margarine, 4 oz bacon and 2 oz of tea. Tea mostly came in quarter pound packets, occasionally in twenty-eight pound foil-lined plywood boxes, to be weighed into whatever quantity was required (4 oz. = approximately .125 kilo). Dried eggs, dried milk and IXL jams from overseas all came in tins. Cheese was also rationed, with heavy manual workers allowed an extra amount. For an old age pensioner the ration for one was barely enough to keep them alive, but green-grocery was never in short supply in the country districts. In those days Co-op shops had no refrigerators, and all fresh meat and bacon etc. had to be kept covered with muslin, sprinkled with pepper, to keep the flies away. Everyone at the Co-op wore a white coat and a white apron, except the van drivers who wore a long buff coat, all of which had to be self-provided.

I became a relief worker, filling in at other branches and occasionally I went out on the bread van as a runner. We delivered from Tansley to Bonsall, Ible, Middleton-by-Youlgrave, Elton, Winster and via Gellia. As relief worker I went to Bonsall, Youlgrave, and Birchover in addition to the other three Darley Co-ops – Little Rowsley, North Darley and Two Dales, and travelled for orders which were delivered by lorries. The van drivers were Fred Hawley, Vic Toft and Ted Dakin. Johnny Mellor from Hartington, Jim Barnes from Matlock and Charles Hollis from Youlgrave drove the coal delivery lorries. Ernest Belfield was the manager at Winster Co-op, Fred Haslam at Bonsall, Mr. Hardaker at Matlock, Eileen Pope at Little Rowsley, Norman Walker at the Two Dales shop and Edwin Billinge at North Darley. Rowsley and Birchover had various managers, as staff kept getting called up into the Services.

We usually cleaned the shops after we closed, ready for morning. All the Co-op shops had thick blue roller blinds for blackout precautions, which were strictly observed. I have fond memories of arriving early in the morning. It was magic to behold the shop area before the window blinds were rolled up – polished brass scales and weights glinting gold, mahogany counters burnished to a rich brown, the glass topped biscuit tins and the chrome fittings of the provisions counter all reflecting the glow of the bare light bulbs hanging from the ceiling. Best of all was the wonderful, exquisite aroma (to call it a smell would be an injustice) of ground coffee, dried fruits, newly cut cheeses, bacon and ham, and myriad other items all blending together to permeate the shop area with a richness rarely found today.

In the early 1940s people still purchased paraffin lamp glasses, soft soap, mouse traps, washing lines and brushes alongside their rations, and flour and yeast. Biscuits always came in tin boxes, vinegar in a barrel, and rough salt in very large blocks for salting down beans. It was an Aladdin's cave. Everything was stocked, from babies' feeding bottles to paraffin, Bile Beans, Carters Little Liver Pills, Castor Oil, Syrup of Figs, Andrews Liver Salts, brands of cigarettes unheard of today, Pelaw shoe polishes, Brasso, Zebo, Black Lead and washing Blues. The Ladies shop also sold a very wide range of goods, from reels of cotton and buttons to hats, lingerie and unmentionables. To work at the Co-op was an education. Some of my workmates included Doug Doxey, Edith Rose, David Wragg, manager Albert Shimwell and Reg Parks, Eunice Birds, and Martha Wall in the Ladies Department. It is lovely to close my eyes and visualise that familiar scene from long ago. I also remember the comforting, all-embracing feel of well-being and belonging that went with the Co-ps. To stand in a modern, soulless regimented superstore is like comparing a spring walk through Lathkill Dale with a journey on a London underground train.

8.30 a.m. pull up the blinds, unlock the door and greet the first customer by name. Come 6 p.m. you had acquired knowledge of everything that was happening around the village, and passed on useful information as part of village life. Pull down the blinds, lock the door and clean and tidy up while the person in charge endeavours to balance the ledgers. All branches opened at 8.30 a.m. and closed at 6 p.m. except for Friday which was 7 or 7.30 p.m., with Thursday half day closing at 12.30. I graduated to travell ing for orders to outlying farms and houses, and when I was 17 acquired a 1927 Ariel 500 motor bike, and a petrol ration. This made travelling a great joy. Driving tests were suspended during the war so I sometimes drove the bread van, as did 17 years old Margaret Seymour, also from Darley.

All Co-op members had a number – my mother's was 925. I think they reached around 5,000. Purchases were put down in your Co-op book in indelible pencil, and paid for on pay day. Tills and ledgers had to be balanced every night (no adding machines or computers then) .We also carried out Co-operative Society Bank transactions for members. At one house I visited for orders lived a retired couple who always had the table laid and a pot of tea on the go, kept warm with a tea cosy supplemented by a large black cat who was always wrapped around the teapot, fast asleep, in the middle of the table. Another dear old lady, poorly sighted, used to ask us to do bits of jobs around her house. We also delivered messages. The butcher, the baker, the milk and paper men, and the postmen, plus the Co-op men who came for orders and delivered them, formed an invaluable contact in the wartime for isolated and lonely people in rural areas. Lots of girls and women took over as the men were called up into the forces. Joan Woolley managed Darley Co-op for a time after her husband Horace was called up, and Elsie Parks took her brother Reg's place at Darley when he too was called up. The Co-op and small shops like the village blacksmith, cobbler and draper in our Darley valley have declined or vanished over the last fifty years, along with the large vegetable gardens and allotments.

The Youlgrave Co-op commenced trading in Mr. George Toft's Fountain Cottage joiners shop, evenings only, in 1870. Mr. Joseph Shimwell from Old Hall Farm,Tom Birds of Hall Farm, and a Joseph Smith were the founders. In 1874 Eli Toft was Secretary and my grandfather George Toft was Treasurer. The Youlgrave and Matlock Cooperative Societies amalgamated and became the Derwent Valley Cooperative Society, which ceased trading in 1968. With the closing of the railway in the same year our valley lost two of its long-time institutions.

Youlgrave Co-op, now a Youth Hostel

CHAPTER 7

MORE MEMORIES OF THE DALES

I have been very fortunate in that the seventy-four years I have spent in our valley has been a lifetime of satisfaction and contentment. I was born on 6th June 1927 at 3 Vineyard Terrace on Darley Hillside.

It is a habit of mine to look out, even on a dismal morning, and gaze around the valley, a truly inspiring sight, and so it has always been for me.

I believe Derbyshire has a unique position in England, with wonderful landscape, villages and hamlets populated in the last century by people whose ancestors lived, loved and worked here for hundreds of years.

Half the population of Britain lives within a sixty mile radius of our county. Darley Dale is blessed by being situated in the centre of this amazing county, astride the major North to South highway through the centre of England. So much scenery, beauty and history at our feet every time we venture out of our homes.

Starting school at Churchtown in 1932 was the beginning of a great love affair and adventure with Darley. At the age of five Churchtown School seemed to me to be in another country, a world apart from my friendly, cosy cocooned world at Vineyard Terrace, Darley Hillside. Every house on the terrace was part of my home with a welcome and an open door. Various pets, including our Irish terrier, Patsy, accompanied me on my visits and at play.

My teacher was Miss Fox, with whom (along with other teachers) I was to be a friend over the next forty to fifty years. We all had our own peg in the cloakroom and our own desk in the classroom. A tin full of small sea shells and alphabet bricks were given to us to play with, also paper and crayons, and a wooden framed slate with a stick of white chalk. We learned to count with the shells and the alphabet with the bricks. I marvelled at the electric lights – we had hissing and popping gas lights at home.

A girl who lived on Vineyard Terrace three or four years older than me, called Janet Allsop, shepherded us to and from school, across the A6 and the railway track four times a day, in all weathers. The classroom always seemed bright, warm, and cheerful. Charlie Hopkinson, who lived on Bent Lane higher up the hillside, started school on the same day as me. We sat together throughout our school life, and eventually became workmates, spending the next fifty-six years in a wonderful friendship. Discipline was strict. Talking in class was not encouraged. Answering back was not even thought of.

The Infant School was separated from the Primary School by a house occupied by Mr. and Mrs. Shaw. Mr. Shaw was the church sexton and caretaker, and sported a walrus moustache. Mrs. Shaw wore a long black dress and button boots, as did several other elderly ladies I knew.

Going to school was a voyage of discovery every day. The journey twice a day entailed walking at least three miles. We went to school and returned home several different ways, exploring, playing games, bird nesting, assimilating detailed knowledge of the countryside. Father, mother and I always went for a long walk on Sunday afternoons around Darley. After two years we moved to the Primary end of the school, beyond the Shaw's house. Boys and girls had separate playgrounds.

In the big school we seemed to be overwhelmed by older boys but I can honestly say there was no bullying. Fights were common place, always arranged, fair and orderly, and taking place at the end of Butts Road where the Derwent Valley Water Board stored their big pipes, with a large audience.

James Charles Bartram, the headmaster, wielded a fearsome cane. The consequence of fighting on or near the school premises was too

Medal and programme presented to the author by Mrs Longson and Miss Newell JP in the tea pavilion, Whitworth Park, on Tuesday 11th May 1937

CORONATION

H.M. King George VI and H.M. Queen Elizabeth

MAY 12th, 1937

Souvenir

Programme

Darley Dale Celebrations

 Price Twopence

HODGKINSON. MATLOCK.

awful to contemplate – I would imagine three or four strokes of the cane on each hand. Each stroke made your hand hurt dreadfully and lasted for a day. The cane was quite short, about 1'6" long and ½" thick (450mm x 12).

Mrs. Rodgers kept a sweet shop next to the school, and many agonising decisions had to be made over spending your penny. Life at home and school was very stable, disciplined and innocent. Animals of all types and sizes abounded, and most of the boys spent some time on various farms. Nature with its births and deaths was no mystery to us.

Poaching rabbits and pheasants was a way of life, also home cured bacon and ham. Lots of people kept poultry and had big gardens. One family, because of their father's serious illness, was very poor and people provided them with surplus fruit and vegetables, and the odd rabbit.

As the journey through my school days progressed we were taught every subject by the same teacher in the same classroom. I moved down from the Hillside to the top of Crowstones Road at its junction with the A6 when I was seven, shortening the journey to school.

The long, hot summer holidays were spent exploring the valley, taking with us a picnic and a bottle of home-made lemonade or nettle beer, which we usually disposed of in the first mile. These expeditions set the scene for years to come. Boys always wore boots and jackets, most wore caps, and the height of ambition was to own a bike, however ramshackle it was. Traditional games were played at various times of the year, conkers, whip and top, hopscotch, marbles, bowling a hoop, skipping and football. Special days were celebrated – Oak Apple Day when we all wore oak leaves, Empire Day and St. George's Day when flags were paraded, Armistice Day, very solemn and everyone observing two minutes silence at 11 a.m. on 11th November, Anzac Day when we had a service to commemorate all the Australians and New Zealanders who served in the Great War. Carnival Days full of excitement, fancy dress and parades with the Band. Wakes Week around St. Helen's Day 18th August, held between the Derwent and the Square and Compass at Darley Bridge. The monstrous gleaming steam traction engine gently rocking and chuffing, with the huge belt that drove the dynamo going click, click. Dozens of coloured lights flashing, and a glorious smell of hot engine oil and smoke. Various noises filled the air – the clang, clang of .22 bullets hitting the steel shields behind the targets, the thump of the wooden hammer on the "Try your Strength" machine, mostly followed by the ding of the bell. Ping Pong balls bouncing out of buckets, swing-boats swishing on the brake beam to stop them – the beam held up by an amazon fairground lady, both the lady and the brake beam bending under the pressure. Every sound intermingled with the fairground organ mounted in the centre of the galloping horses, and the thud of the wooden balls against the canvas behind the coconut stall. A truly exciting atmosphere for the young people of the valley to enjoy, and if they were lucky spend their one or two shillings (5p and 10p).

On Saturdays, when I was around ten or eleven years old, my friend Geoff Sellers (who lived next door) and I received sixpence each (2½p). We caught the bus to Matlock, tuppence single, threepence return, and went to the matinee at the old picture house down Dale Road, Matlock. It was tuppence to go in, leaving one penny to spend on sweets or a glass of pop, or, if we had decided to walk back to Darley, an extra penny to spend – then we could have both sweets and pop.

We often walked back across the other side of the Derwent, via Darley Bridge, exploring, or over Hackney and down to Ladygrove when the weather was good. Life was rich and full. I was around twelve years old when I had my first ride in a car. Mick Morris, the furniture man, gave Geoff Sellers and I a lift to Matlock. Very few people had a car in the 1930s.

There was a very select Youth Club, run by Eric Griffiths the Rector's son, in a room in the old curate's house next to the rectory of St. Helens. The criteria for joining seemed to be a church connection, choir member etc., and Charlie and I decided to join the choir probationers. I could sing well but the discipline of attending practises and church was too much for me. I had attended the Hillside Chapel up to the age of twelve. Charlie stayed on. It seemed life would carry on in its settled manner for ever.

I was twelve years and ten weeks old when talk of war arose in August 1939, and my eldest brother John, who had left the Navy in 1938 after service, some served in China, was recalled to the submarine base at Gosport All the boys at school were excited by the talk of war. Brother John lived on Darley Hillside with his wife Bertha, and four years old son Geoffrey. Bertha gave birth at home to another son (John) on 1st September. I called in to see her and the baby on Sunday morning 3rd September and we sat and listened to the Prime Minister, Neville Chamberlain, broadcast to the nation at 11 o'clock. He made the fateful statement that we were now at war with Germany. A way of life vanished at that moment.

School was suspended. Eight or nine days later, towards dinner time, I saw our postman, Wallace Young from Stanton Lees, coming up the path. My mother went to the door. He broke the news to her that brother John had been killed by "an accidental explosion" and asked mother to go with him to Bertha to be with her when he gave her the telegram containing the grim news.

I went with my distraught mother and the postman up the Hillside to Bertha and her new baby son. I could not comprehend that my brother John was dead. My world went to pieces. Another School from Manchester had come to stay in Darley Dale and go to our Churchtown School, I, along with lots more children and parents went to the school. There seemed to be hundreds of nervous girls there, clutching suitcases, each with a label and a gas mask case. I was told they were evacuees and were looking for people to take them in.

We were issued with our gas masks and taught how to use them. Ration books were issued and Identity Cards, my number being R BTD/185/4. We had an air-raid warning exercise in which everyone went and sat in St. Helen's Church. Windows were blacked out, and street lights turned off.

Towards the end of September School was resumed, shared with the Lady Barnes' pupils. We spent half a day doing gardening, nature walks or games and half a day in class. In one month my life had turned upside down.

The Winter months were dark, gloomy and austere as shortages of food and goods became widespread. Bus services were curtailed, young men I knew were called up into the Forces. After the Christmas holidays a number of the Lady Barnes Girls School evacuees did not return. Life seemed to be settling down again and I was coming to terms with the war. Little did I know what was to come.

A feeling of confidence was in the air. Britain was holding its own in the war with Germany. Spring arrived and with it the shock of the German onslaught on France, a sense of disbelief that Britain was about to be defeated on the continent. Once more our school was disrupted.

Churchill became Prime Minister. The Home Guard was formed, and more Special Police, and more Air Raid Wardens were recruited. The Whitworth Institute became a base for soldiers evacuated from France.

In July the Headmaster, Mr. Bartram, gathered the school together and informed us that the ringing of Church bells would be the signal that we were being invaded by the Germans and paratroopers would be dropped. He told us that when we heard the bells, no matter where you were or what you were doing you must go home at once and stay there.

My brother Jim was called up for National Service in the May of that tumultuous year which led to great anxiety in our family. I was thirteen on 6th June 1940.

When the Home Guard was formed my other brother Clifford joined. They were equipped with a limited number of Lee Enfield .303 rifles, and on Sunday mornings shooting practice was held at the butts above the end of Cavendish Road, Matlock.

I went up to Cavendish Road on my bicycle to meet my brother and see if I could join or help. I was posted to the butts target area to assist target marking. My first session in the butts became deeply engraved in my memory. Home Guard men were instructed in the handling of the rifles. Some of them had fought in the First World War and were familiar with and competent in handling the rifles. Others had never seen one before.

Several men and I walked from the firing position to the target area. We carried red flags and targets about four or five feet square, plus long poles with a circle of cardboard nailed on one end, painted black on one side and white on the other. The targets were fastened to pairs of iron frames. The frames worked on a counter-balanced system, one up and one down. The target went up about eight or nine feet. The trench the target frames were in was about eight feet deep and ten feet wide, several hundred yards away from the firing position. When we had fitted the targets to the iron frames and all was ready we took down the red flags which were mounted on tall poles. A whistle blew and moments later the crack of a rifle rang out. Standing in the trench with our backs towards the firing position we gazed up at the target, looking for the small hole about the size of a large pencil. You then placed the marker over the hole for a few seconds. The target was pulled down, to be replaced by its twin. We then pasted a square of white paper (black if it was a bulls-eye) over the hole.

I think there were about four target frames in the trench. I was amazed to hear the bullets thumping into the earth behind the target and occasionally bits of stone and earth ricocheted into the trench. It was very scary, and very busy. I found that listening to the hiss of the bullets and the thump of them hitting the earth bank a few feet above your head made one want to crouch down. After a stated time whistles were blown.

The red flags were then put back and after a short time we returned to the firing position, passing our replacements. After several Sundays, as a reward I was shown how to handle a rifle and allowed a few shots. I had an airgun at home so knew how to aim. Children were not allowed to join the Home Guard.

By the beginning of October, with all he excitement of the Battle of Britain (which according to the propaganda of the time we were winning by a large margin) fears of an invasion receded so I stopped going to the butts.

Britain ran on double summer time, dark in a morning, light at night. The Germans started bombing cities at night. The night they bombed Sheffield I cycled on to the moors and watched, spellbound, at the searchlights, flashes, and firework-like sparks in the sky from the anti-aircraft guns. I also watched the bombing of Derby. It was much the same and with a strict blackout imposed the flashes of exploding bombs and the spark-like explosion of the anti-aircraft shells were easily seen. Shrapnel collecting became a pastime, railwaymen and lorry drivers picking it up to give to their children as souvenirs. My father was an engine driver and he sometimes went to London, to Kentish Town marshalling yards. He lodged there before returning with another train back to Rowsley. He told me how frightening it was when a bombing raid was on. The only oasis of light in our valley was the Railway Sidings which for safety reasons had to be lit unless an air-raid was imminent. Oranges and bananas vanished sweets became very scarce.

As a child a lot of information was passed down to me by adults, the whereabouts of walnut and hazelnut trees, the best mushroom fields, which rabbit warrens to set nets in and how, and easy places to tickle fish. All the boys knew where the most isolated fruit trees were. One had to be very careful on these poaching and plundering expeditions as penalties were very harsh. The local Police were actually our friends, giving us friendly warnings when we overstepped the mark.

Soldiers occupied the Whitworth Institute and its grounds, Smedley's Hydro and several other places. Darley roads became dangerous as the R.A.S.C. driver training school was based at the Whitworth. Army lorries, mostly in small convoys ushered by motor cyclists, practised day and night.

After the winter air-raids on Manchester some evacuees, who had gone back home in the phoney war period of early 1940, returned. Education at Churchtown School was very sketchy because it was grossly overloaded with pupils. Holidays were extended. Brother Clifford was working at Patons and Baldwins factory, Smedley Street West, Matlock. This factory was commandeered by the Ministry of Supply to house a tap and die factory from London called Lehman, Archer and Lane. Clifford enquired about a job for me for when I left school at the end of July, or whenever. We had one week's holiday at Whitsuntide at the end of May 1941 and I was offered a week's work with the factory engineers over the Whitsun holidays. I started work there at the end of May, one week before my fourteenth birthday, and because of the colossal state of turmoil at school, and in the country in general, I never returned to school. The working hours came as a shock, from 7.45 a.m. to 5.45 p.m. I was living at Crowstones Road, opposite the Grouse Inn. The Silver Service bus left the Whitworth Institute at 7.10 a.m. and I almost always had to run to catch it. The bus, after dropping people off in Crown Square, Matlock, carried on up Bank Road to Patons and Baldwins. Buses in the wartime had the seats placed end to end around the inside of the bus, leaving a large space in the centre for people to stand in. All the lights inside were disconnected, but the conductor had a shaded light strapped to the money bag to enable him to see the money and work the ticket machine. I went home at 12 oc. mid-day on Saturday but the others worked longer hours and Sundays.

The only recreation facilities were the picture houses at Matlock, Bakewell and Wirksworth. I went to the pictures two or three times a week. The boys of central Darley met early on Sunday afternoons and went exploring the countryside or neighbouring towns. A bitter blow came in late 1941 because of shortage of fuel. Bus services ceased at 9 p.m. from Matlock, however a local train ran just after 10 p.m. from Matlock to Darley Station, making it a long walk home.

To my delight in 1940 our valley was declared a low flying area and since then I have seem almost every type of military aircraft zooming around the valley, from old bi-planes to the latest A10 American war planes.

Everyone listened to the radio and read the newspapers. As the war years dragged on older friends were called up for service. Families you knew lost loved ones. Most of the men from Darley were scattered far and wide. Soldiers were everywhere, food was scarce, soap a luxury, travel difficult.

I was fortunate to be at the right age, twelve, when war broke out. The next six years of hardship became normal to me and others around my age group. The progression of the war, with all its scarcities, disasters separations and turmoil became part of everyday life. The fighting may have finished in 1945 but the wartime way of life, rationing, curtailment of transport, lack of housing, shortage of recreation dragged on into the 1950s so the return to normal living and time was protracted, unlike the sudden shock I received in September 1939.

I was taken ill and spent my fifteenth birthday in the Whitworth Hospital. I never went back to the factory as I could not stand being imprisoned there for ten hours every day, and I went to work for the Derwent Valley Co-operative Society. There were no recreational facilities whatsoever at that time apart from the pictures. Through the war years, from 1941 to its end, the boys from central Darley met most nights and after dinner on Sunday at the shops at the bottom of Broad Walk, from where we all went to the pictures or just talked. Sunday was expedition day. We went for long walks or caught a bus to a neighbouring village or town, nearly always between eight and twelve of us. We were sometimes mischievous but never got into serious trouble.

Going over Darley Bridge one Sunday we noticed the barge-like boat of the River Board moored to a tree by a chain, locked to a large staple driven into a tree. We all got hold of the chain and heaved and the staple popped out of the tree. Finding two or three branches to use as poles we took off up the river. About one hour later, as we glided back alongside the tree with the intention of mooring the boat a very irritable man, the river bailiff, emerged from behind the tree, shouting and carrying on. Someone jumped off the boat on to the bank and held the chain while we all got off. Edward Moorby, probably the youngest of the party, was the last to get off. By this time the bailiff was becoming very agitated, shouting and leaping up and down. Whether he slipped, or received a slight push, I don't know, but he and Edward Moorby were suddenly chest deep in the river. Edward now (for a young boy) became very voluble, shouting at the bailiff, who was shouting back. We pulled them out of the river with one of the branches. By this time they were both leaping up and down so we rescued Edward, took him into an adjoining field, stripped him and wrung out his clothes. It took ages for him to cool down! A couple of days later we heard the barge was stuck on the weir at Artists Corner, below High Tor. The village policeman, P.C. Thorpe, asked us if we had enjoyed our cruise and gave us another warning.

We boys made our own recreation throughout the war. The state of war, after three or four years, became the norm. Soldiers were everywhere, Airmen in a different blue uniform from the Hydros turned Hospitals, sat in the Hall Lees Park, American soldiers sight-seeing, A.T.S. women everywhere. I loved watching American Army convoys belting down the A6, sometimes with a black driver waving.

Because Darley Valley was a low flying area every type of plane zoomed around. One day fifty-two Flying Fortresses passed reasonably low over the valley in a staggered formation. The noise was tremendous – I remember it was a Sunday afternoon. War was a seven days a week job.

Two of the boys about six months older than me got a job driving a three-ton petrol engined Bedford lorry for Shirley & Proctor or the Express Dairy, collecting milk from farms in the Peak District to the Express Dairy at Rowsley, and later in the day or at night taking the milk to neighbouring towns and cities. I helped Mr. Hallows, the farmer from Cherry Tree Farm, Darley Hillside, with their milk round on Sunday mornings, and they taught me to drive. I was sixteen, nearly seventeen. There were no driving tests in the wartime. Sometimes I went on night runs with the boys to deliver 720 gallons of milk in ten-gallon churns to Sheffield, Nottingham, or Nestles Dairy at Ashbourne. Sheffield was my favourite place to go to. There were no sign posts, a complete blackout, trams with pinpoints of lights, cruising down the middle of the road, bombed out buildings, and Air Raid Wardens. Steamy fog hung over the city on damp winter nights and people scurried across the roads. The only other vehicles on the road were a few heavy goods vehicles, buses and Army lorries. I loved journeying on the lorries. Some Sundays I did not go on Hallows' milk round. Instead I went to the Express Dairy about 7 a.m. and cadged a lift with one of the drivers in return for helping him to load the churns. We usually got back before dinner time.

I got to know the highways and byways of the Peak District quite well.

By this time most of the boys wore overalls and bits and pieces of Army uniforms. Decent clothes were hard to come by and severely rationed. In the winter I wore one of my father's railway overcoats, very warm. Coal was rationed and father and I cut logs with an old crosscut saw. Mrs. Hallows from Cherry Tree Farm, along with Mrs. Pearson and my mother (both from Vineyard Terrace) and several other ladies had worked in Stancliffe Quarry in the First World War when men were scarce.

Before they left the farm around 6.30 a.m. to go and milk the cows in the dairy behind Stancliffe Yard, Mrs. Hallows' two sons Jack and Charlie used to prepare breakfast. They had a large cast iron basin shaped pan. Dripping was smeared around the inside, several half inch thick pieces of home cured ham went on the bottom, then a couple of slices of plain bread, then more ham with a couple more slices of dripping spread bread on top again. The pan was placed in the side oven of the huge black-leaded coal fired range, and the fire banked up. When we had finished with the cows, cleaned down, cooled the milk and washed the churns and the two gallon delivery cans (each with a pint and a half-pint ladle inside hung from two hooks) it was breakfast time. We loaded up the van and went back to Cherry Tree Farm. As we went in the farm kitchen a most delicious smell met us, taste buds tingled in anticipation. Remember it was wartime and a usual breakfast was dried egg scrambled on toast, or bread and jam, perhaps porridge.

Three dinner plates were produced, and the gorgeous, savoury concoction cut into three immense slices. A knife and fork, and a pint mug of tea with a couple of saccharins (nicknamed 'depth charges') and breakfast began. The ham fat had become so tender that you could squash it against the roof of your mouth with your tongue and feel it dissolve. All the breakfast literally melted in your mouth. On a cold, dark winter's morning it was like being in paradise – lovely food, warmth and a glorious aroma pervading the room. It made the war and its hardships seem very far away.

People, young people especially like myself, became almost immune to bad news because it came so often. I realised later in life that we knew and expected the world to turn upside down every now and then, either on a personal or a national basis. Plane crashes in the area, army convoy smashes like the one down Sydnope Hill when several soldiers were seriously injured and at least one lost his life. People in the street casually asking if you knew the Battleship Hood had been sunk with only three survivors, or Singapore had fallen. Neighbours telling you that the so and so family had lost a son. Boys I knew, a bit older than me, were called up into the forces.

I received occasional letters from the Middle East, and from a friend who went into the Royal Air Force. I went to the funeral of a local lad who had died in the armed forces in Britain and was sent home to Darley to be buried.

The people who I really felt sorry for were the very elderly who had suffered the hardship of the First World War and were now mostly living alone in small cottages high on the valley slopes. They had only food rations for one, could not garden, had no telephone or access to a bus. The only thing plentiful was shortages of everything necessary to life – food, warmth and comfort.

The war ended in 1945 but there were to be several more years of shortages and hardships. There were also some joys – loved ones returning from the ends of the earth, families reunited, a stop to the flow of bad depressing news.

After the war everything was a bonus, especially when one realised what could have happened in the autumn of 1940. We are all so lucky. I believe that people much older and more settled than myself found it much harder to cope with the stress of wartime Britain 1939/45 because they had tasted the horrors of the 1914/18 war. War produced the full range of emotions in people but as I have realised in later life a child growing up in wartime accepted the life we led in those far off days as normal. Such is the resilience of the young.

Just after the war with the exception of Firth Rixson's factory the valley was much the same as it was when I was a child. Our valley had changed very little in the two or three hundred years before 1848 when the advent of the railways commenced, a first period of change that was to last a hundred years. The Darley of 1950 still bore a resemblance to the 1850s with its traditional hamlets, industries, agriculture, and limited commuting by train and bus. Despite a hundred years of migration into the valley people still knew one another, working and playing together. Most of the local industries were large employers of labour.

Darley was a self contained community of mostly manual workers Access to the big cities was available if one had the time and the money. Most men worked Saturday mornings. Women had to work hard at home cooking, washing, cleaning, sewing, with no or few labour saving appliances. Electricity only came to the valley seven years before the Second War. Transportation was by bus, train, bicycle or feet.

Our valley began to experience a different way of life in the 1960s. What had always been presumed to be its nucleus and lifeblood – the railway, vanished overnight in 1968. It was not the catastrophe everyone imagined it would be, a saviour was available – the car.

People now worked outside the valley, and people from away considered Darley as a great place to live. Hundreds of dwellings sprang up, their occupants commuting to work in other towns and villages. Agriculture practically vanished, local industries employed fewer workers as labour saving machinery took over. Leisure and shopping facilities had so much more to offer in large towns and cities. In spite of living in densely populated pockets and working shorter hours fewer people knew their neighbours. The South side of our valley has changed very little, and is still a close-knit community. It also has a caring and tidy aspect to it.

Over the last forty years the North side of the valley from Matlock to Rowsley above the A6 has gradually attained an atmosphere of neglect, probably because of the demise of the local roadman and the intense use of impersonal road machinery. Weeds and self-set trees obtrude into the highways, which are more used by vehicles today than ever before. What a difference a few roadmen, like Bill Salt, Bill Hopkinson, Joe Webster, George Tomlinson, Bob Ainscough would make, men with a pride in their work. Surface water drains have become run-down, roads and fields flooded. One great blessing is that in the last few years we have had no very severe frosts and snows. The climate of the valley has become more mild.

It is inevitable that our valley's population will continue to expand as it has everything people desire in a place to live. I am so pleased I was born before the age of television and the universal use of the car. I was privileged to pass my young days away exploring almost every nook and cranny of it which endowed me with a sense of belonging and a comforting feel when I return from a journey away. I still rejoice when I gaze around the valley I know so well. Just to watch the sun rise over Darley Hillside on a spring morning, casting its rays over South Darley and flooding the fields with a golden sheen, cannot help but fill the gloomiest miserable person with delight. Then in the evening when the day is almost spent, the sun lights up the crest of the North East valley side. Stanton top, with its craggy outline is back-lighted silver, the birds cease to sing, shadow covers the valley bottom, a miriad twinkling street lights glow, and peace and tranquility shrouds our valley. May it stay that way for the next generations.

EPILOGUE

Lead mining was first recorded in the area in the reign of Emperor Claudius. The Barmote Courts, which regulate the lead mining industry, are believed to have been held continuously for approximately one thousand years. My Toft ancestors and their descendants, who have lived in the Youlgreave area since the early 1500s, have long been associated with the lead mining industry and its Barmote Courts.

I believe the Grace which is said at the Great Barmote Courts, is a fitting finale to the book.

"Eternal and ever blessed God, who has made us heirs of many ages, and set us in the midst of many men,
Deepen our gratitude for Thy blessings, as we have received them,
From our fathers, our benefactors, and our friends.
May we never forget the kindness which surrounds us in the present,
Nor be unmindful of the treasures we inherit from the past,
But having a lively sense of our debt to our neighbours,
And a loving remembrance of departed generations,
May we reverently carry forward the work of the ages,
And daily endeavour, as faithful Stewards, to enrich the same,
By a good conversation, and a godly life.
Through Jesus Christ, Our Lord, Amen."

Lewis R. Jackson

CHAPTER 8
SOUTH DARLEY AND DARLEY DALE LOCAL HISTORY WALKING TRAILS

The Darley Dale Trail is based on a Darley Dale Society leaflet by the late Ernest Paulson published in conjunction with the Arkwright Society in 1976.

The South Darley Trail is by the Darley Dale Society members Irene Wright, Sheila Slack and the author.

DARLEY DALE TRAIL

Prelude to Trail 1.

Darley Dale, similarly to South Darley, is composed of a series of hamlets. Pre-1980 they stretched from Rowsley road bridge over the Derwent to the east end of Smedley Street at Matlock. With the formation of parish councils Northwood, Tinkersley and Little Rowsley were separated from Darley Dale, but can never be separated from our valley. At low level are Churchtown, the Church without a town, Two Dales formerly Toadhole, and Little Rowsley. Higher up on the eastern hillside slopes, on the spring lines receiving all the sunshine and sheltered from the bitter north-east winds, are historic Northwood and Tinkersley, Darley Hillside, Hackney and Farley. More modern hamlets, or should we call them housing estates, are Central Darley, Darley House Estate, and the estates of Hooley Town and Stanton Moor View. All these settlements are home to over six thousand people.

These small communities grew up almost independently of each other linked only by the parish church, St. Helen's. Near to the church is Churchtown School, built in 1847 and currently with a roll of 150 children, and the mis-named Abbey House, the supposed site of the 1066 home of Edmond of Erle in Normandy, who took the name Edmond of Darley, and from whom sprang a world-wide dynasty of Darleys. Some of his descendants built the Mayflower, the Seaflower and the Bonaventura, which played such a large part in the birth of America. Associated with these communities at different times in their history are a number of notable people; the brothers Daniel, Edward and James Dakeyne of Toadhole, the inventors of the disc engine, a form of water turbine, and Sir Joseph Whitworth (1803 to 1887) who, in 1856, purchased Stancliffe Hall, are perhaps the most easily remembered. Sir Joseph in particular was a major influence in the growth of Darley Dale, even though his philanthropic plans were never fully realised. When he bought the Hall Whitworth was already well known as an inventor and successful manufacturer of machine tools and as the advocate of a standard and uniform system of screw thread, but his own greatest achievements and the growth of his own Manchester-based company into a major industrial enterprise producing steel and armaments as well as machine tools, lay in the future.

Today Whitworth is remembered as one of the first great production engineers and as a prophet of standardisation, precision and mass-production. Business apart, the Stancliffe Estate became Sir Joseph's main interest and he applied to its management the same rational methods he had developed in engineering. Whitworth set about restyling and landscaping his new property, but it was some twenty years before he finally took up permanent residence (1874). Throughout this period he was a regular commuter between Manchester and Stancliffe. Until the opening of the through route to Manchester in 1867 he had to make the journey via Ambergate and Sheffield. It is no wonder that he took an active part in canvass ing the idea of extending the Midland line to Buxton.

The railway was an important influence in the growth of Darley

Dale; the line from Ambergate and Derby which passed through Darley was opened as far as Rowsley in 1849. The first station was probably a small wooden building, but this was replaced by a more permanent structure designed by Joseph Glossop in 1872 by which time with the opening of the line to Manchester in 1867 Darley had acquired easy access to every part of the British Isles. With the development of the Rowsley depot and sidings Darley Dale became a railway centre. Railwaymen's families are proud of their past and keep their memories alive.

Darley, by the end of the nineteenth century, was also a considerable tourist centre. The grounds of the Whitworth Institute were popular with sunday schools, Bands of Hope, women's organisations and working men's clubs, who came for picnics and days in the open air from large cities in the region, notably from Manchester. In the grounds of the Institute there was a large stone-built tea room, a boating lake, tennis courts, swings, a bowling green, and inside a museum, library and art gallery.

A glance at the older editions of the 6 in. O.S. map suggests another facet of Darley Dale's past. At the end of the last century several hundred acres of hillside were devoted to nurseries. In 1895 James Smith is reported as having "300 acres of ground where may be seen, growing in native luxuriance, the trees, shrubs, heaths and flowers of every clime from Indus to the Pole". The nurseries stretched through almost 900 ft of altitude from the Nursery appropriately named Siberia at nearly 1,100 feet, down to Wi llow Grove at river level behind the Church. Now most of these 300 acres have reverted to forest, moorland and bog. The industry flourished in soil and terrain which was particularly suited to heathers, heaths and conifers, but its development owed a great deal to the drive and organisation of the Smith family.

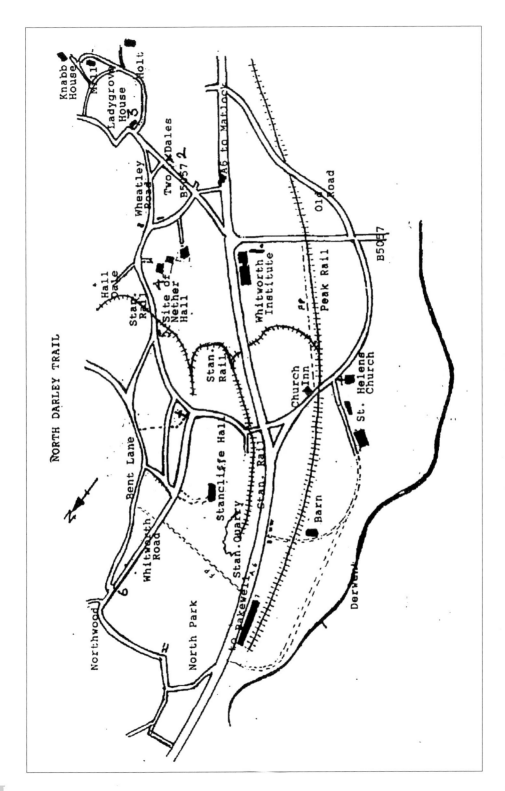

NORTH DARLEY TRAIL

DARLEY DALE TRAIL, PART 1 –

DISTANCE APPROXIMATELY 2 MILES

The trail begins at the Whitworth Centre (point 1) which stands where the B5057 Chesterfield-Winster road crosses the A6. Adequate parking can be found at the Whitworth Centre. The Whitworth Institute and Hotel was designed by Olive and Atcherley of Manchester and opened in 1890, three years after Sir Joseph's death. It had been conceived as the focal point of a model village and was to have been part of a college housing primary and secondary schools, craft apprentice workshops, a library, recreation rooms, a gymnasium and a swimming bath, a museum, a lecture hall and staff hous ing. Little of this was built during Sir Joseph's lifetime but his trustees were able to complete the Institute and the Whitworth Hospital. Whitworth's plans helped change the face of Darley, and had he lived to see their completion there is no doubt that the area around the Whitworth Institute would be occupied by his proposed model village. If one stands in front of the Institute facing the building which once housed the National Westminster Bank (now a chemist's shop) on the left of the road to Two Dales, almost opposite the Whitworth on the A6 can be seen a fine iron milestone, half buried in asphalt.

Before moving off towards Two Dales on the B5057 it is worth considering why there should have been two banks in this area. The answer is that Williams Deacons (now Royal Bank of Scotland) was in association with the Savings Bank run by the Whitworth Trustees and had already established their premises. Parr 's took over the interests of the Dakeyne Bank and set up their own premises in competition in a wooden building on the other side of the road. Parr's were part of the original group which subsequently founded the now defunct Westminster Bank. Later the wooden hut was replaced by the present building (chemist's shop).

Cross the A6 and walk a little way towards Two Dales. Twenty yards along the road to your left is the Underhall sheltered housing complex. A little further, near the junct ion of the five roads, is a nursery business connected with the Smiths, the Forest Nursery Garden Centre (where refreshment can be purchased). Continue along the road to Two Dales, passing on your left typical stone-built terraced houses and on your right will be seen the former school built by public subscription in 1871 for 100 children, now Hayes Bakery. Another 70 metres along, on the same side, set down from the road, is the Old Reading Room (now three dwellings).

Arriving at the little bridge (point 2) notice on the left the Dakeyne House (previously the Co-op) and on the opposite side the former Blacksmiths Arms and its Smithy (both now dwellings). Two more public houses, the Nags Head and the Plough Inn, were located in the area of the bridge and the covered-in Hall Dale Brook. The Nags Head was demolished but the Plough Inn (another Dakeyne house, built in 1751) remains

Further along at the foot of the hill, where the road turns right to Ladygrove, stands a rectangular Georgian mansion (point 3). This was built by Edward Dakeyne in 1796. Taking the turning to the right, Ladygrove Road, and passing Holt Farm on the right, there is a small group of houses. A private drive leads from here to Holt House, the main Dakeyne residence, a fine Georgian building. On the left hand side of the road is Ladygrove Brook with a grassed bridge over it. This contains the Derwent Valley aqueduct pipes feeding water to Nottingham, Derby and Leicester. Continue up the road alongside the brook and you will come to Ladygrove Mill. Higher up the brook are the three dams which supply water to the Mill. Ladygrove Mill (formerly Dakeyne's Flax Mill, and now the home of Johnsons Millers) was the site of three vertical water wheels, the famous hydraulic engine and latterly a water turbine. The tall building at the rear, which houses the pipework and fed the wheels and the turbine, is still in situ. There was a building (now demolished) on the south side of the road opposite the Mill which housed the Dakeyne disc engine.

One can now retrace one's steps to the B5057 or go beyond the Mill, taking the steep narrow road to the left, past the Mill yard. On the right stands a modern bungalow, the site of Loscoe Row, fourteen mill houses, now demolished. Carry on up the hill and Knabb House, the original home of the Dakeynes, is on the right. Keep left and take the next sharp left, Denacre Lane. This will return you to Ladygrove Road. Retrace your steps, again passing the drive to Holt House which housed the Dakeyne's Bank of Darley Dale until 1881.

Cross the B5057 and take the narrow road past the Plough Inn and ascend Wheatley Road. At the road junction Wheatley House, a three-storey Georgian building, is on your right, one of the former homes of the Smith nurseries family. Turning left is a cottage at the junction, built in 1703 by Robert Barker. The Barkers were sheep farmers, and in the garden there is a short pillar with their brand carved on it. Chrichton Porteous, the Derbyshire author, lived here for many years, and moved to the new adjoining chalet bungalow in 1974. Note the old Nursery bell, called Clam Danel, which regulated the workmen's hours in the former nurseries.

Proceeding down Park Lane the building adjacent to Clam Danel was the former offices of James Smith's Nurseries, now a dwelling. Below the old offices is a small housing estate named after Crichton Porteous. This was previously the site of the James Smith & Sons packing sheds and dispatch area. The next drive, on the right, leads past several large dwellings to Darley Hall, now a Residential Home .

Continue down Park Lane, passing on the left the stone late-Victorian dwellings to the B5057. Retrace your steps to the Whitworth Centre.

DARLEY DALE TRAIL, PART 2 – DISTANCE 4 MILES

Start again from the Whitworth Institute car park. Cross the A6 and take the B5057 towards Two Dales, turning left up Park Lane at the five-way junction. At the junction with Wheatley Road and Hall Moor Road turn left past Wheatley House, the former home of the Smith nursery family. The road climbs steeply. Notice the point where the Nether Hall drive crosses the road and continues to the right, up Hall Dale. Continue on the road, and to the left and round the corner from the horse trough is the humped and pitted field where the Nether Hall, old Darley Hall, once stood (point 4). The modern Darley Hall can be seen at the bottom of the field.

Looking across the valley to the left is Oker Hill. To its right the road from Darley Bridge winds up the hill to Cross Green and Wensley, and to the right again are the tall chimneys of Enthovens lead works and its associated tips. In the trees in the valley bottom lies St. Helen's Church. On the skyline diagonally right you will notice the television mast. Close by, to the left, just below the horizon can be seen Stanton Stand. This is also known as the Earl Grey Tower and was erected to celebrate the Reform Bill of 1832. It is placed supposedly in such a position as to be visible from the estates of the Dukes of Rutland and Devonshire.

Morton's Estate (Broad Walk) in the near right foreground and on this side of the valley, can be seen from this point. These rows of houses were built by Morton of Bakewell between 1924 and the 1930s. They were well built with frontages of local Darley Dale (Stancliffe) stone, specifically for housing railway workers who were employed at the huge marshalling yards which were, during this period, being extended towards Rowsley. A few of the original families still live there. Between Morton's Estate and Darley Hall is the Parkway Estate, mostly constructed in brick and tile and built between 1950 and 2000 by various estate builders. The portion next to Morton's Estate was formerly the site of the 1960s John Turner school and playing fields.

Continue along Hall Moor Road. The house on the left at the bottom of the dip was formerly Sir Joseph's Laundry. On the right you will notice great blocks of waste stone. These come from the Hall Dale Quarry and form part of the railway track bed. The track from the quarry crosses the road diagonally and continues downhill through a plantation (point 5). This is the route of the standard gauge railway which came from the quarry and ran down to the the masonry yard at Stancliffe works and beneath the A6 trunk road to meet the main line railway. The line was originally laid in 1903 but was taken up in the 1914-18 war and sent to France. It was later relaid and continued in use until just before the Second World War. Past the track the road meets Long Hill on the right. Keep left and go straight on for 50 metres then pause at the bottom of the small incline and observe the ruins of Cherry Tree Farm on the left, which the Hallowes family farmed for many years. It was a very old farmhouse, demolished in 1963, and all its fields have now been planted with trees. Stancliffe standard gauge railway ran just below it. Go forward a short distance and just before Moor Lane on the left note the large horse trough on the right. Keep on Hallmoor Road where there are some eighteenth century cottages to the right as you ascend the short slope to Vineyard Terrace on the right. Next, on your left, is the old track Gill Lane, then another group of old cottages on both sides of the road. A few yards further along, on the left, can be seen, adjacent to the road, the roof of View Cottage, once the home of Joseph Whitworth's Agent, Mr. Dawson. Next is a fairly new dwelling called Saunters Nook – the original name of Foggs Hill. At the end of Hallmoor Road, looking downhill to the left, is the entrance to Stancliffe Hall. Foggs Hill, before Whitworth Road was made in 1874, ran down to the Hall to join the old road from Northwood to the Church.

The high stone walls of Whitworth Gardens are in front of you; turn right up Foggs Hill. Springfield, once the home of the Misses Fogg, then the home of the Derbyshire family of nursery men, is on the right at the top of Foggs Hill. The Derbyshire family still reside there. Turn left to continue along Bent Lane. On the left are the high stone walls of Sir Joseph Whitworth's former kitchen gardens. Sir Joseph was a man who valued his privacy. In his time the cottage on the right, Dunelm, belonged to Jake Millward. When Whitworth built the wall in front of the cottage, to ensure his privacy, Millward retaliated by building himself a lookout post high up his field where he could observe Sir Joseph's activities, much to Whitworth's annoyance. Continue along the road passing several more old cottages to the end of Bent Lane. At this point the Trail divides with the option of going down Northwood Lane (the longer route) or turning left down Whitworth Road, the shorter route (point 6).

SHORTER ROUTE

Continue down Whitworth Road, observing on your right the start of Sir

306

Joseph Whitworth's coursed stone walls. The field entrance at this point marks the beginning of the original road to Darley Church, past Stancliffe Hall and through Sir Joseph's Lane.

Near the beginning of the high stone walls (which hide Stancliffe Hall on one side and the kitchen gardens on the top side) a stile will be found on both sides of the road. Note the date adjacent to the left hand stile, 1883. This marks the beginning of the building of the walls surrounding Sir Joseph's kitchen gardens. Go through the right hand stile and into the field, known as North Park. Observe the clumps of trees to the right, planted to shelter Sir Joseph's pedigree cattle and horses. The old wooden building on the right, with a new roof, is the last vestige of Sir Joseph's stable. Follow the path which descends steeply to the A6, cross the track which is the last vestige of the pre 1830s main road and emerge opposite the end of Firth-Rixson's factory. This was built on the railwaymen's recreation ground in the early part of the Second World War for armaments manufacture as a so-called "shadow factory" away from its parent company in Sheffield, where there was greater chance of damage by enemy action. Turn left and look out for a stile on the right, about 300 yards along the A6 before Holmfield House. The path is signposted "Churchtown" and leads to Darley Church. (If wet one can continue along the A6, turning right down Church Lane and over the level crossing to St. Helen's Church).

The footpath crosses the rail track and just after a barn turns left along the track of the old Derwent Lane which ran from the bottom of Northwood Lane to Darley Church. The path continues along the farm drive past Abbey House, probably the site of the original Darley Hall. From Abbey House it is a short distance to the school, the earliest part of which was built around 1848, with an extension in 1911 and a further extension (the portion with the french windows) in 1933.

Next there is an old cottage, once the sexton's house, and then a larger dwelling called The White House, rebuilt from an old beer house called The White Horse. When The White Horse lost its licence in the mid 19th century it became a farmhouse and post office. Before 1840 when Darley Parish extended two miles in all directions from the

Church, the White Horse was the centre for those who came to morning service and stayed to Sunday School. The original day school, on the left hand side of the entrance to the Rectory, had 15 to 20 pupils in 1792. The Sunday School had four masters teaching under the supervision of the remarkable Thomas Gregory, who held his post from 1782 to 1824 and died the following year aged 93. He was landlord of the Crispin Inn, now the nearby Church Inn, parish clerk, leader of the church musicians, bell-ringer and schoolmaster. Nevertheless his Church activities were so numerous that the inn was always shut on Sundays. Opposite the east end of the Church is Rectory Farm, of which the house and buildings date back to 1607. The small building at the far end near the Rectory gates is of considerable age and was once the house of the Rector. A tablet in the south gable carries Latin inscriptions and B.E. 1607 (Brian Exton, Rector).

St. Helen's Church and the ancient yew tree have been frequently described and literature is available inside the church. The tower was built by Sir John de Darley in the 1300s and the eight bells are well known to ringers far and wide. To the left of the west door is a weathered bas-relief of two deer and to the left of the porch, incorporated into the present building from an earlier structure, is a dark Saxon knot-worked stone. The nave was widened in 1854 but the walls of the chancel and the transepts are 14th century, though the chancel has been re-roofed and a door and window cut into it. Below the walled up Norman windows are the graves of several 17th and 18th century rectors and their families. The sundial on the south transept was erected by Sir William Wray. In those days the old road made a wide sweep passing close to the east end of the chancel. The stone coffins between the main door and chancel are interesting. The smallest, with its cover, was found under a column in front of the pulpit when it was straightened in 1877 – it contained a child's skeleton. Near the chancel door is a circular stone slab variously described as a millstone, a grindstone, a lid to a Roman sacrificial urn, and, what seems most likely, the base of an old preaching cross. Such crosses were usually stone plinths or obelisks situated at a focal point where visiting clergy would preach. If this was a preaching cross it may have stood on the green which used to stretch beyond the north gate of the church as far as the Crispin, now the Church Inn.

You may reach the inn by walking from the church north gate towards the former level crossing of the old Midland line from Derby to Manchester. Having crossed this, immediately in front of you is the "Butts House", built on the site of the old archery butts, and behind this is the Church Inn. If you did not come down this way take time to glance up the road past the inn and see the semi-detached houses built for the workers of Sir Joseph Whitworth's estate. Over the level crossing turn immediately right, and take the footpath which runs parallel to the railway. Leave this footpath at the end of the football field into Whitworth's celebrated park. Note the bed of the old boating lake, the cricket pitch, and the wide variety of fine trees. In the centre is an obelisk with metal insets describing his life and achievements. Sit here a while and try to recall in imagination the visitors of former days, the bands of happy trippers, the sunday schools and workingmen's clubs from Nottingham or Manchester, Stoke or Sheffield, listening to the band, watching the cricket match or a Punch and Judy Show, rowing peacefully round the lake, or just enjoying the trees and hills.

ALTERNATIVE ROUTE FROM POINT 6 – AN EXTRA MILE

Instead of turning sharp left down Whitworth Road carry straight on, passing Lumb Lane on the right and go down Northwood Lane. Note the water trough on the left. The Lane then splits. Take the right hand fork, following the bend round to the left. Note the cottage on the right, and its windows, then several more old cottages dating back to the 1600s.

Rejoining Northwood Lane, the old house on the right hand corner is the former Northwood Farm, which is reputed to be haunted. Carry on down the lane, which turns to the right, down a very steep incline. There were no houses on Northwood Lane from the 1600s cottages and Northwood Farm to the A6 until after the First World War. Over the brook at the bottom is Cotehillock Lane which leads to the old hamlet of Tinkersley.

At the north end of the bridge wall, on the bottom side, is an old sign/mile post. Cotehillock Lane was known locally as Gypsy Lane as gypsies camped here up to the 1920s. Matlock Transport now occupies the land to the right. The lane formed part of the original main road from Rowsley to Matlock. After the second world war the building on the left of the road was built as the Northwood Village Hall. It then had a period as a Night Club, and at the present time is unoccupied. Carry on down Northwood Lane to the A6. Across the A6 stands a pair of semi-detached railway houses of 1873 on what must be the shortest lane in Darley Dale, Derwent Lane. The lane, which went over the fields to the church, went out of use in the early 1900s, except for this short stretch to a level crossing for farm traffic, named Nanny Goat Crossing.

Carrying on along the A6 southwards the complex of industrial buildings on the right, and the three dwellings on the left were the garage and homes of the haulage firm Toft and Tomlinson, Ltd. The garage was called Unity Garage. On the right adjacent to Firth Rixson's steel works is Riversdale House, another former home of the Wall family. At the southern end of the factory, opposite North Park, we re-join the trail.

NOTE

At the junction of Church Lane and the A6, opposite Cosim Works, stands Sir Joseph Whitworth's West Lodge. This was at the southern end of the old road from Northwood, which went past Stancliffe Hall. Sir Joseph made this the main entrance to the Hall, and, no doubt to impress his visitors, had this elegant dwelling designed in the French style. His drive meandered through what is now Stancliffe Quarry, alongside North Park to Stancliffe Hall. The drive then continued forward from the Hall to Whitworth Road at the bottom of Foggs Hill, with a branch going off through a tunnel under Whitworth Road to his walled kitchen gardens.

SOUTH DARLEY TRAIL – INTRODUCTION

South Darley lies on the western slopes of the Darley valley of the River Derwent. It is composed of a string of hamlets commencing with Snitterton in the south, Oker village, Okerside, Cross Green, Wensley, Cowley and Darley Bridge adjacent to the Derwent. In years past these were typical small self-contained North Derbyshire hamlets with long histories. Snitterton, Wensley and Cowley were manors in the Domesday Book.

Limestone predominates on this side of the valley, with a huge mound of shale known as Oker Hill. The northern tops of the valley slopes are capped with gritstone at Stanton Lees and Cowley.

The valley side from Cowley to Rowsley is very sparsely populated. The Duke of Rutland's previous hunting lodge and associated farm Stanton Woodhouse is the only settlement between Cowley and Great Rowsley. The name South Darley only came into being in the 1840s when it became a parish in its own right. Many notable families have lived in the area. Cowley was held by the King at the time of the Domesday Book, and was reputed to be the site of a hunting lodge. The Wendesley family had a reputation for being very warlike and took part in many battles. Peveril Castle at Castleton was under their wardenship for a time and the Wendesleys were Knights of the Shire six times.

Wensley, like Snitterton, has a long history of lead mining, and the fields behind it are pock-marked with old mining ventures. Cross Green is the area to the south east of St. Mary's Church and the old main road from the ford at Darley Bridge to Winster and beyond. Above Winster runs the Portway, the Bronze Age trackway passing through our county, with stone circles and burial mounds close by. Oker Hill is believed to be the site of a Roman station, as many Roman coins and some artefacts have been discovered on the hill. Snitterton and its manors are linked with the Millward family. A sough, or drainage tunnel, from the lead mine on Masson hillside passes under Snitterton to emerge into the Derwent below the iron railway bridge over the river. Traces of medieval ploughing are visible on the hillside slopes above the hamlet. The area from Snitterton to Cowley Knoll was chiefly agricultural and lead mining until the 1930s. Agriculture and the legacy from lead mining, lead smelting, are still the predominant industries today.

One of the notable people of South Darley was Joseph Taylor, who through his connection with the Eagle Brewery of Manchester, was a great benefactor, contributing towards the village school and a row of cottages called, after his brewery, Eagle Terrace. He also provided a reading room in 1891. In St. Mary's Church there is a Burne-Jones window above the altar dedicated in 1891 to Joseph and Sarah Taylor. William Wordsworth visited the area and became acquainted with the story of the Shore brothers, Will and Peter, and the tale of the lone tree on top of Oker Hill. Peter and Will, who at that time owned the hill, decided to each plant a sycamore tree on the top. Peter left the area to travel overseas and sadly soon died. Strangely his tree also died. Will's tree thrived and became a prominent landmark in the valley. Wordsworth was so inspired that he wrote the following sonnet.

"Tis said to the brow of yon fair hill
Two brothers climbed, and turning face to face
Not one more look exchanging, grief to still
Or feed, each planted on that lofty place
A chosen tree: then eager to fulfll
Their course, like two new-born rivers they
In opposite direction urged their way
Down from the far-seen mount. No blast might kill
Or blight that fond memorial; the trees grew
And now entwine their arms; but ne'er again
Embraced these brothers upon earth's wide plain:
Nor aught of mutual joy or sorrow knew
Until their spirits mingled in the sea
That to itself takes all – eternity"

St. Mary's Church is noteworthy in that it is not aligned east-west in the traditional manner, probably because of the confines of the site, with its steep drop at the rear.

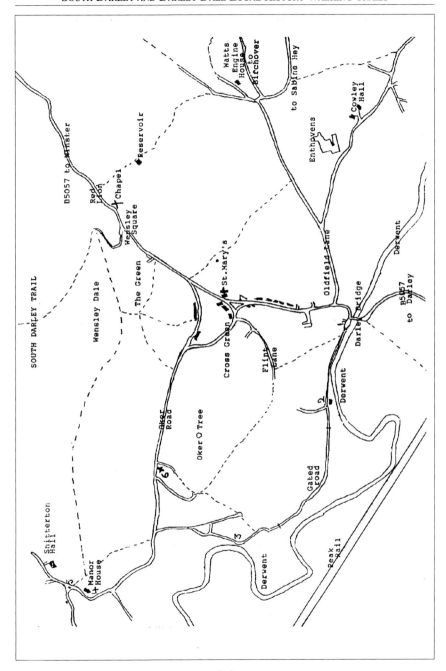

THE SOUTH DARLEY TRAIL, PART 1 –

DISTANCE 2½ MILES (4 KILOMETRES)

The trail begins at Darley Bridge (1). There is a small public car park on the south side of the bridge, at the junction of the gated Wenslees Road with the B5057. The vicinity of the car park is a good place to observe the bridge itself, and its mixture of two pointed and three rounded arches. It is said that many years ago there were two more arches on the north side. The north river bank is now very steep and has probably been infilled to help accommodate the bridge approach. A glance at the wide shallow river bed shows why this was the site of the ford which preceded the bridge.

Proceed along the Wenslees gated road for about 400 metres to a small group of buildings (2). The second building on the left, now clad with stone, is actually a wooden dwelling house. This substantial building formerly stood 100 metres up the private drive from the gate on the right, and was moved to its present position early in the twentieth century. It was clad with stone and extended in the 1990s. Continue along the gated road for about 600 metres to where the road runs alongside the river. It was in this area that Captain Ward built his mansion (3) in the 1920s but no trace of it now remains. This end of the road is called Aston Lane.

Pass Sitch Road, a cul-de-sac, on the right and turn left onto Snitterton Road. 150 metres along the road on the left stands a pair of large houses. The one on the right is the home of the celebrated wildlife artist Pollyanna Pickering. Be careful of traffic coming round the bend as you make your way towards Snitterton old Manor House (4).

In 1541 Snitterton old Manor House was the home of John Dakyn, who had family ties with the Wendesleys of Wensley and the Fitzherberts of Tissington. At the rear of the house, according to Tilly, there is reputed to be a gable of the original Manor House. If true this must be part of one of the oldest dwellings in our area. The property was owned in the 1700s by Richard Arkwright.

One hundred metres towards Matlock, just before an acute bend in the road, a track leads off to the right (5). At the junction of the road and track there is an iron ring set in a large stone which was used for fastening bulls to be baited by dogs. Walk up the surfaced track to Snitterton Hall. Several great families have held Snitterton Hall. The Shirleys held it after the Conquest of 1066, and later the Sacheverells and Millwards. Snitterton Hall is on the boundary of the Low and High Peak Hundreds. It is difficult to get a good view of the Hall, which is a pity because it is a fine building. It was the home of the Derbyshire and Staffordshire Bagshawe family in the 1900s. An absolute wealth of history lurks in Snitterton.

Retrace your steps back to the Aston Lane junction. If fine and dry there is a footpath from near the bullring to Aston Lane. Take the road now called Oker Road leading towards Wensley, passing Oker Lane, the old Methodist Chapel on the right (6), then Will Shore's (of the tree) Lane. After about 400 metres Kirby Lane is on the right. Walk along Kirby Lane, passing Flint Lane on your right. This area is known as Cross Green. Keep right and join the main road B5057 (7).

It is now a short walk down the hill, passing the Three Stags Heads inn to the car park.

SOUTH DARLEY TRAIL, PART 2 –
DISTANCE 2¼ MILES (3.6 KILOMETRES)

Good footwear is essential for this walk. Leave the Darley Bridge car park, passing through the old hamlet of Darley Bridge. Note the old Post Office and the Three Stags Heads inn on the left, opposite Oldfield Lane. Ascending the hill the site of the old Ivonbrook Sawmill is on the right (now Ivonbrook Residential Home). The long row of stone semi-detached dwellings on your right, built in the 1930s, is called Eversleigh Rise.

The first part of the trail is rejoined above Eversleigh Rise (7). At the bend in the main road the village school is on the left. Note the Bell House on top, restored in 1989. The adjacent Village Hall, built in 1952, plays a very important part in the life of South Darley, and is home to the Parish Council. St. Mary's Church, with its carillon of eight bells and Burne-Jones window, is opposite the Village Hall There is a steep drop into a small limestone dale at the rear of the church. This dale was the site of the dam which powered Ivonbrook Sawmill. The fields on the right contain several old lead mines, including the Barley Close Mine.

Proceeding up the hill towards Wensley, on the left-hand side of the road above the junction of Oker Road and the B5057 is the site of the Toll Bar and its cottage (now demolished). Opposite is Forge Cottage and the old blacksmith's shop, now a cottage. Further above, Homelea, on the right-hand side was once the Post Office – note the dovecote openings on the east gable. On the west end gable is a built-up window, a relic of the window tax days. In 1696 Parliament imposed a tax on every dwelling house, except those not paying church or poor rates, as follows: –

For every house with fewer than 10 windows, 2s. (two shillings). From 10 to 20 windows, 6s. 20 or more windows 10s. This tax was increased six times between 1747 and 1808, but reduced in 1823. In 1808 by a gradually ascending scale, the charge on a house with 180 windows reached £93. 2s .6. with an additional charge of 3s. on every window over 180. The tax was repealed in 1851 and a tax on inhabited houses substituted.

Note the Footpath on the right-hand side of the road which ends in a water trough. Opposite Homelea is Wensley Hall, once the home of the Wall family. The footpath below leads to the Green. The Green was the site of the old Wendesley Manor House. Wensley Square above was the site of a bull ring, also the Post Office and The Crown inn. On the top side of the Square is a house with a window made from glass bullions. The narrow lane leading off the Square leads to Greenstile Cottage and also to Wensley Dale. Greenstile Cottage was the first place of worship for Methodists in Wensley in 1812. Pause here for a moment and look at the view – Oker Hill in the foreground with Hackney, Matlock, Riber and beyond in the distance.

Immediately above the Square, on the right-hand side is the old two-storey barn-like limestone building which was once the Reading Room and Dance Hall. On the left-hand side approximately 30 yards above the old Reading Room is a pair of large limestone dwellings which were once the Earl Grey public house.

Around the corner stands the present Reading Room built in 1891 with money povided by Joseph and Sarah Taylor. Joseph Taylor was a local brewer and benefactor, and many of his descendants still live in the village. The inscription above the Reading Room door translates "Sweet is the place of one's birth". Opposite the Reading Room stands Wensley Methodist Chapel. The Local Preachers Mutual Aid Society was founded here, and each October Methodists from all over the country gather here for a service of remembrance.

Above the Reading Room is Eagle Terrace, built in 1893 – the Eagle Star Brewery was the name of Joseph Taylor's brewery. Across the road is the Red Lion, the only public house left in the village, the Crown Inn in the Square having closed a few years ago. Immediately after the Red Lion car park is a footpath. This is three eighths of a mile (600 metres long) down to the Watts Engine House and Shaft. This is a steep descent and good footwear is advisable. (If weather conditions are bad an alternative is to return to Darley Bridge car park and proceed by car up Oldfield Lane behind Enthovens works to the junction with the old road to Birchover to view the remains of the Watts Engine House and Shaft).

Take the footpath which passes a reservoir mound at the hill top, and the only reasonably flat field where Wensley Football Club had their ground. As the path continues down it passes several old capped leadmine shafts. In the valley bottom cross the brook and follow the track to the right. A slight diversion to the lcft leads to the remains of the Watts Engine House, built in 1860. Watts shaft was part of the Millclose Mine, which had been worked since the 1600s.

Leaving these remains retrace your steps and take the stile next to a gate, bear left, passing the old Birchover Road. At the footpat sign proceed down a walled track for 200 metres towards Sabine Hay, and at the sign "Slippery Steps" on the right carry on down the old stone footpath, worn hollow by miners' boots for over 100 years. This footpath eventually becomes a tarmac road and a few metres after the Kawecki Billiton (Enthovens) building pass over a stile, and on reaching the Stanton Lees road turn right. Next to Enthovens works is historic Cowley Hall, another home of the Wall family for many years and once owned by Sir Richard Arkwright. This Hall is now used by Enthovens as offices.

Beware of traffic as there are no footpaths in the area.

Continue along the road, passing Enthovens Lead Smelting Works. The Works originated in Lea and moved to South Darley in 1933. This was also the site of the last of the Millclose Mine operations. Opposite the Works are spoil heaps composed of calcite and limestone, the residue from the lead ore separation plant. Continue on this road, passing Bridge Farm on your left, and return to the car-park at Darley Bridge.

ACKNOWLEDGEMENTS

Ron Slack
Bill Stringer   Millclose
Percy Smith   Bakelite
David Westmorland and Charles Maddocks   Johnson's Mill
Geoff Sellers and Ken Dabell   Shands
Reg Street and Jim Taylor   Stancliffe Works
The late Ernest Paulson
Peter Woolliscroft
The Waters and Lowe families
Mrs. Mary Jackson
Frank Blair
Ken Wareham
Bill Salt
Bill Erskine, Barmaster of the Barmote Court
My wife Barbara and daughter Lesley, for typing, proof-reading and patience.

and the many others who have willingly shared their knowledge and memories with me.

BIBLIOGRAPHY

Bode, H. *James Brindley an illustrated life of James Brindley.* Shire Books 1973.

Ford, TD and Rieuwerts, J.H., editors *Lead Mining in the Peak District* 4th edition. Landmark Publishing, 2000.

Glover S. *The history, gazetteer and directory of the County of Derby* 1829.

Pendlet;on, J. *A history of Derbyshire* 1886.

Tilley, J. *The old halls, manors and families of Derbyshire* 1892.

Willies, *Lead lead mining* Shire Books 1980.

Smith, A. W. *Notes on St. Helen's Church* 1951.

Wigfull, P. *The Dakeyne Mill.*